BeesKnees #2:
A Beekeeping Memoir

Volume Two: Days 101 - 200

The Journey of a Beginning Beekeeper

Fran Stewart

BeesKnees #2: A Beekeeping Memoir
Fran Stewart
© 2019

All rights reserved. No part of this book may be used or reproduced in any manner whatsoever without written permission from the author, except by a reviewer who may quote brief passages in a review.

Cover design by Darlene Carter

ISBN: 978-1-951368-02-9

This book was printed in the United States of America.

Published by
My Own Ship Press
PO Box 490153
Lawrenceville GA 30049

myownship@icloud.com
franstewart.com

To the students in my memoirs classes

Yes, you see? It is possible.

Books by Fran Stewart

The Biscuit McKee Mystery Series:

Orange as Marmalade
Yellow as Legal Pads
Green as a Garden Hose
Blue as Blue Jeans
Indigo as an Iris
Violet as an Amethyst
Gray as Ashes

Red as a Rooster
Black as Soot
Pink as a Peony
White as Ice

A Slaying Song Tonight

The Scot Shop Mysteries:

A Wee Murder in My Shop
A Wee Dose of Death
A Wee Homicide in the Hotel

Poetry:

Resolution

For Children:

As Orange As Marmalade/
    Tan naranja como Mermelada
        (a bilingual book)

Non-Fiction:

From The Tip of My Pen: a workbook for writers
BeesKnees: A Beekeeping Memoir - Volume 1
BeesKnees: A Beekeeping Memoir - Volume 2

Introduction to the Second Hundred Days

If you've read the first volume, you already know I still hadn't gotten my bees installed by the end of Day #100. Why not? Because I started the blog in October—and that's NOT the time to introduce a new hive.

"Why didn't you wait to start blogging?"

I'm glad you asked. It's because I wanted to share the whole journey with you.

Whether you choose to plan well ahead as I did, or simply get your bees and get going, I wish you the best and honey-sweetest jaunt imaginable.

I hope you're enjoying this journey through the BeesKnees.

And remember, you don't have to a beekeeper to enjoy my experience.

> --Fran
> from my house beside a creek
> on the other side of Hog Mountain GA
> Summer 2019

 ## Day #101 To treat or not to treat
Friday, Jan. 21, 2011

This is so cool! I went back to do some re-reading in *The Complete Idiot's Guide to Beekeeping*, and found yet another reason—very clearly expressed—for why it's not a good idea to feed bees sugar water (except when the bees are getting first established).

Bees apparently self-regulate the size of their colonies based on the amount of food available. When there is less food (in the form of nectar and pollen) the queen slows down on the egg laying. When they stop rearing brood for a time, it interrupts the life cycle of the diseases and parasites that grow in the brood chambers.

When beekeepers feed the bees constantly from early spring to late fall, the bees never get that "message" that it's time to slow down, so the parasites keep right on multiplying. *Then* the beekeepers find it necessary to treat with antibiotics like Terramycin and Fumadil.

Do you really want to eat honey that has antibiotics in it?

Even the use of so-called *natural* treatments (like dusting with powdered sugar) interferes with the microbial culture in the hive. Just because something is natural, doesn't necessarily mean it's a good idea. Stiglitz and Herboldsheimer asked us in *The Complete Idiot's Guide* to imagine "using the oil of the poison ivy plant as a massage oil." Hmmm.

I'm more and more glad every day that I've decided to let my bees simply BEE.

BeeAttitude for Day #101: *Blessed are they who let us BEE what we want to BEE, for they shall help populate the world with healthy pollinators.*

One thing Fran is grateful for right now: *My new wood carrier, a birthday gift from my massage therapist, Karen Krotz*

Fran Stewart

 ## Day #102 Lions and Tigers and Bears! Oh my!
Saturday, Jan. 22, 2011

Yesterday I called to ask about being tested for allergy to bee-stings. The first thing the woman asked was, "Have you ever been stung by a bee?"

"No."

"Then we don't need to test you. The only way you'll show an allergy is if you've already been stung once."

I knew that. I remember a high school science teacher who was also a part-time farmer. Once, he brought in the head of a cow he'd slaughtered and we got to . . . well, I won't go into the fascinating details since you might have just eaten breakfast. But he also taught us about allergies and how they worked.

Now, I *have* been stung before, but never by a bee. There was this wasp once, when I was maybe seven years old. My family had stopped at a little refreshment stand near the Lorelei Rock on the Rhine River. I swear I wasn't doing a thing to the wasp, but he took offence and attacked the inside of my right elbow. I probably screamed, but all I really remember is looking down at that gorgeous wasp-waisted body—well of course it was *wasp*-waisted—and wondering how something so beautiful could be so mean. Then the lady behind the counter asked my father in pantomime (our language facilities were strictly limited) for his handkerchief. She doused it in cognac, which astounded my mother greatly, and bound my arm in the odorous white fabric. After that I don't recall much of the trip except my generally whiny attitude.

When I was in my thirties I had a run-in with some ground-nesting yellow jackets. Yuck!

And then there was the time my three-year-old granddaughter trooped into a hornet's nest. I flew into action, dragging her away from them and beating them away from her. I was so concerned about her, I never noticed the multiple stings I received. *Not* one of my favorite memories.

But bees? Never. Of course, once I'm opening their hive next summer, they are liable to show some concerns. Every beekeeper I've talked to has said, "You *will* get stung." Okay, but I still bet the bees will be nicer about it than those other critters were.

Hornets and yellow jackets and wasps! Oh my!

BeeAttitude for Day #102: *Blessed are those who help the injured, for they shall reap what they sow.*

One thing Fran is grateful for right now: *That dear lady at the roadside stand all those years ago.*

 ## Day #103 Ah-ha! A Solution to My Dilemma
Sunday, Jan. 23, 2011

All this time I've wasted grumbling about not having a table saw—and yesterday the light dawned. I called H & L Bee Farm, the people I bought my five-frame garden hive from several months ago, and asked if they would be willing to sell me the hive components so that I could put them together and paint them myself.

The answer? Yes!

So, I'll pick up those extras (one cover, one deep hive body, and five honey supers) when I get my bees in eight more weeks or so. By the time my bee colonies are ready to split, I'll have happy new homes ready for them to move into. And I'll be able to use top bars instead of foundation, so I'll be able to harvest delicious comb honey. If you're wondering what I'm talking about, go back to Day #1 [*in volume 1*], where I explain what foundation is.

Now I just have to decide what color to paint the new hive. Any suggestions?

BeeAttitude for Day #103: *Blessed are those who are open to inspiration, for they shall bee pleasantly surprised.*

One thing Fran is grateful for right now: *My old high school buddy, Ellen, who said she'd send me some Macadamia Nut Honey from her sister-in-law in Hawaii.*

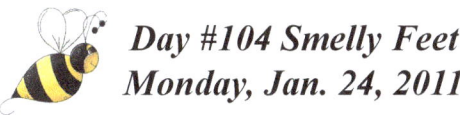 Day #104 Smelly Feet
Monday, Jan. 24, 2011

Queen bees have smelly feet, and that's what keeps their workers happy.

(c) Yelloideas Photography

The tarsal glands on the queen's feet ooze with pheromones (chemical substances) that ebb and flow. The mandibular glands in her mouth do the same thing. Nobody's figured out precisely how many pheromones are present, but it is known that they are precise indicators of the queen's health. Changes in the balance of pheromones let the worker bees know what shape their queen is in. If she smells right, she's okay. If something goes wrong with her, her feet change their smell and the workers know they have to do something.

The attendant worker bees constantly groom the queen, and this spreads the queen smell throughout the hive. The bees are so sensitive to the smell of their queen that when a queen is disabled or is removed from the hive, the workers all know it within minutes and spring into action to correct the problem.

As any bee can tell you, you gotta have those wonderful, informative, smelly feet!

BeeAttitude for Day #104: *Blessed is she who knows (nose) what's she's doing, for she shall, like us bees, be productive.*

One thing Fran is grateful for right now: *The New American Shakespeare Tavern in Atlanta, where they present original practice Shakespeare year-round—that's Shakespeare's plays the way they were presented at the Globe Theatre.*

 ## *Day #105 Gargoyle and Mistaken Identities*
Tuesday, Jan. 25, 2011

I finally sent in that order! Soon I'll have a bee brush (you know about those because I've talked about them before in this blog) and a frame perch (so I won't have to set frames on the ground) and an Italian hive tool (skinnier and lighter-weight than the regular ones) and a hive net (so I won't risk letting loose bees roam around my car when I pick them up from the bee farm). And a few other things as well.

So, I'm going to go make some lists of things I still have to do to get ready for my bees. While I'm doing that, you can check out Gigi Pandian's blog. *[2019 Note: Gigi's gargoyle blog is no longer active.]* She's a photographer who shares her photos of gargoyles. Like this one:

© *Gigi Pandian*

She explains that *Le Penseur (the Thinker)* is one of the most famous gargoyles in the world, but it's not really a gargoyle. Why not? A gargoyle is supposed to be the end of a gutter. It generally spews rainwater out of its mouth. But Le Penseur just sits there and thinks. Not a gutter-end. Therefore, not a true gargoyle.

This started me thinking about how many people blame bees for stinging them, when most likely it wasn't a bee at all, but rather a wasp, hornet, or yellow-jacket. If you think *Le Penseur* is a gargoyle, are you more likely to think a hornet is a bee? Well, you won't make that mistake anymore – not with Gigi and Fran around!

BeeAttitude for Day #105: *Blessed are those who share their photographs, for they shall bring joy to others, and that joy shall be reflected back to themselves.*

One thing Fran is grateful for right now: *The birds flocked in my front yard.*

p.s. I have Gigi's permission to use her photograph.

Day #106 The First Bee of the Season
Wednesday, Jan. 26, 2011

Last Monday, I walked around the car and saw a honeybee (!) perched on the car just below the passenger-side window. The first bee of the season.

My first thought was that, with nothing in bloom at this time of year, I'd better whip out some sugar water to feed the little girl.

Fortunately the reasoning part of my brain took over. You see, if I had put out food that she and her hive mates could eat (and she definitely would have told them about it), then they would be fooled into thinking that this one slightly warm day was an indication that spring was here. They probably would have speeded up egg production, which would have resulted in an increase of baby bees *before* the plants in Georgia were ready for them.

That would mean either that I'd have to keep feeding them sugar water (NOT good for them – it's like raising a child on nothing but potato chips) or else all those excess bees would die off. As it is, the bee looked at the **yellow spots** on my car, decided they weren't edible, and flew off. I have no idea where she came from, but you have no idea how happy it made me feel to see her.

Here's a picture of my yellow-spotted car right after she won a trophy at an antique car show one rainy day last year. I wasn't competing, but EllieBug was definitely the only car there dressed in polka dots, so Gail Dunn, the organizer of the show, gave us a trophy for "the car with the most spots."

EllieBug's Trophy Dec. 2009

Fran Stewart

Now you're going to want to know why I put spots on my car . . .

It's so I can find her in a parking lot.

BeeAttitude for Day #106: *Blessed are they who look for spring, for they make the spring appear.*

One thing Fran is grateful for right now: *Pete Ogg from Texas. She emailed me late on Day #105 to ask where the blog was for the day. I'd left it in draft form instead of hitting the publish button. So, it came out about 17 hours later than it should have – but, thanks to Pete, still made it on the right day.*

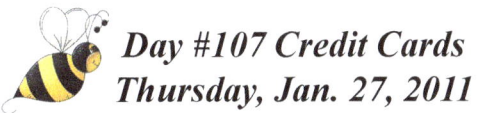 ## Day #107 Credit Cards
Thursday, Jan. 27, 2011

I have one credit card, and only one. I pay off the entire balance every month. I've taken Dave Ramsey's *Financial Peace University*. I believe in absolute fiscal responsibility. I keep very good financial records.

That said, this month I goofed. When my credit card statement came, I found a $10 charge on there that I swore I could not possibly have made. I called USAA and explained to them that I'd never been to that particular hotel, which was way too fancy ever to charge only $10 for something; they reversed the charge, but they gave me the phone number of the hotel so I could check to see if anyone had counterfeited my card. I called the hotel.

Some nice young man spent time and effort researching the charge and finally told me that it was a valet charge. Ohmigosh! I'd completely forgotten a friend of mine needed to go to downtown Atlanta that particular day so she could attend an awards luncheon. For various reasons, she couldn't drive, so I acted as chauffeur and ate lunch with her. When I went to get the car after the lunch, I didn't have any cash with me, so I put the valet charge on my credit card, but then my friend handed me $10 in cash and took the printed receipt.

Sum total of it was that I forgot to enter the charge in my spreadsheet. Grrr… These programs only work if you actually sit down and put in the information. Anyway, I then had to call USAA back again so they could re-reverse the charge.

Credit is never an issue with honeybees. Maybe that's because they're smarter than we are.

BeeAttitude for Day #107: *Blessed are those who pay attention to what they're doing, for they shall be less confused in the long run.*

What Fran is grateful for right now: *The two people at USAA and the one at Twelve Atlantic Station who graciously spent their time helping me.*

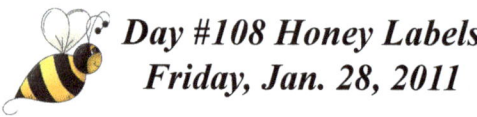 Day #108 Honey Labels
Friday, Jan. 28, 2011

I had so much fun yesterday unpacking my order from Brushy Mountain Bee Farm. I'd ordered (among *many* other things) labels for my jars of honey. I don't even have the bees yet, and I'm already anticipating a wonderful harvest—probably because I spoke with a young man at Staples when I was buying a new printer. He said his uncle planted clover, and his bees doubled their honey production. Guess what I'll be planting around my garden in the spring? *Quick, Frannie, order some more seed!*

At any rate, I'd ordered a template to go along with the labels. Now I have labels that say:

Bees Knees
Beekeeping
Lawrenceville GA
16 oz.

Imagine that wording on this label from Brushy Mountain Bee Farm:

BeeAttitude for Day #108: *Blessed are those who sell honey, for they shall have more money to buy plants that we bees love.*

One thing Fran is grateful for right now: *Patra, the woman who delivers my mail each day*

Day #109 Gwinnett Environmental & Heritage Center
Saturday, Jan. 29, 2011

If you've been reading my blog from the start, you may recall that I was inspired to keep bees after speaking with various beekeepers last September at the Gwinnett Environmental and Heritage Center. It's that kind of place—they pull together fascinating people and fascinating information in thought-provoking, fun exhibits.

© BluePeak.net

Yesterday I dropped by there to see *Your House, My House.* What fun! I got to step inside a Navajo hogan, a Malaysian stilt house, and a Fijian M'bure. I also got to try to put the roof on a Mongolian ger (rhymes with dare). That one was a model about 3 feet in diameter, and I struggled to get poles threaded into a wooden circle and attached to leather brackets spaced around the circular wood frame wall. After it was together (sort of), I had to place a canvas top over it and get the hole in the canvas to line up with the wooden smoke hole. I will admit that it was lop-sided when I finished, but I still had a good time. Give it a try sometime.

© *BluePeak.net*

Fran Stewart

As I was leaving, I stopped at the front desk to thank them and to tell them that I was starting beekeeping as a result of that exhibit they'd had last year. The woman called out the Education Program Coordinator, Brian Sterne. Seems he's a beekeeper, and he has a top bar hive, which is precisely the kind I want to build over the summer. He gave me a lot of good advice on how to craft the top bars.

Beekeepers are very special people, ready to share their knowledge and to encourage newbies in the field.

BeeAttitude for Day #108: *Blessed are the exhibit-makers, for the delight they bring shall filter back to them.*

One thing Fran is grateful for right now: *Holtkamp Heating & A/C Inc., the sponsors of "Your House, My House" at GEHC.*

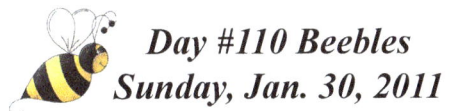 Day #110 Beebles
Sunday, Jan. 30, 2011

Okay. I admit that there are times I get absolutely **zany**. This is one of them. One of my favorite toys used to be a giant bubble-maker, a huge plastic loop that my kids could dip in a bucket of soapy water. The worm-like giant bubble trail that wove around behind them when they rotated or trotted across the yard always made me laugh.

Where does the zany come in? I was just thinking about my bees. If I ever try to blow bubbles on my back deck after the end of March (which is when I'll get my honeybees), I'll run the risk of having the bees fly into the bubbles, which will then make them . . . groan . . . beebles.

Sorry 'bout that.

BeeAttitude for Day #110: *Blessed are those who laugh with their children, for – years later – they shall be filled with joy when they remember.*

One thing Fran is grateful for right now: *The Friends of Smyrna Library and the Atlanta Chapter of Sisters in Crime, who put on the Murder Goes South conference yesterday. I attended, and it was loads of fun.*

p.s. **A word of warning**: *don't blow bubbles around bees. The soap would coat their wings if they flew into one, and you'd end up hurting the beebles—I mean the bees..*

Fran Stewart

Day #111 White Wax and Cardboard Boxes
Monday, Jan. 31, 2011

This past week has felt like a bonanza. Four separate orders of beekeeping supplies were delivered to my door. Four boxes of magic. At least it feels like magic to me. I now have a hive perch, an "inspector's jacket," three beetle blasters, a bee brush, an Italian hive tool, and a whole bunch of other goodies. Yeah!

One of those other arrivals was a one-pound block of white beeswax. As I get my top bars built, I'll be applying a thin line of beeswax along the length of each bar, so the bees can use it as a roadmap for where to build their combs. I'm not sure the wax is an absolute necessity, but the bees I've ordered were all raised on man-made foundation. These sheets of plastic are stamped with a raised pattern of hexagonal cells that have been coated in beeswax. The bees follow that pattern in drawing out the comb (making each cell deep enough to hold eggs, baby bees, nectar, honey, pollen—all the necessities of life in a thriving hive).

But I want my bees to form their own comb, with no plastic guiding them. I've heard and read that a line of wax centered on the bottom side of each top bar will at least get them started in the right place. After that, it's up to Mama Nature. The problem with drawing comb completely all by themselves is that it takes a tremendous amount of effort and resources on the part of the worker bees. And, before they can draw the comb, the hive has to be warm enough to keep the wax malleable as they form it.

It will be my job as a beekeeper to make sure there is enough room in the hive so the bees don't have to store their nectar in the brood chamber (because that would mean the queen would have no cells in which to lay her eggs).

My cats are delighted, because the four orders mean cardboard boxes for them to hide in. I have an empty beehive in my living room, boxes everywhere for the cats, shelves overflowing with books I love, music on public radio. Life is good.

BeeAttitude for Day #111: *Blessed are the beekeepers who give us enough room to grow, for they shall find honey in abundance.* This beginning beekeeper hopes that is right . . .

One thing Fran is grateful for right now: *My new hive net, so I'll be able to enclose the nuc and the package I pick up in South Georgia in eight weeks. I don't particularly want a bunch of stray bees getting out of the nuc on my back seat and flying around the car for several hours while I'm driving home.* [**2019 Note**: Remember this entry for when I finally get around to picking up my bees.]

Fran Stewart

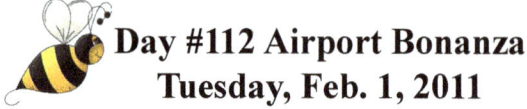

Day #112 Airport Bonanza
Tuesday, Feb. 1, 2011

I had a long wait at an airport in Florida once, when I was on my way back from a speaking engagement at Edison College. I got to talking with the woman sitting beside me, and she's turned out to be a wonderful resource. Jill Sensiba knows a lot about plants, and whatever she doesn't know, she knows how to find out.

Jill bought all my books (bless her!), and after reading *Indigo as an Iris*, the fifth in the series, she wrote me an email that included this section:

Regarding forgiveness, I was recently touched by a TV show where a priest was leading a forgiveness group, and one of the members of the group said, "He doesn't deserve my forgiveness." The priest reminded the group that forgiveness is a gift we give ourselves. Now that I've heard it, it seems so obvious, but I hadn't really thought of it that way before.

From a karmic viewpoint, I see forgiveness as the form of Divine Love that loosens the karmic ties that keep us bound together until we can learn to untie them. I thought you did a marvelous job in Indigo *describing the personal struggles we all have when we are ready to move on and let go.*

One time I was thinking about someone who had wronged me, and the image that I got was that I sat holding on to one end of a ball of twine, and the other person had the ball. He walked around, unconcerned and unaware of either my anger or my need for him to "get what was coming to him." Because I wouldn't let go of the twine, I'm the one who ended up all wrapped up in the twine as the other person just went about his day. Eventually, I was so wrapped up, I couldn't move.

As I came to this realization, my Inner Guide showed up with a large pair of scissors, and managed to cut away all the loops of twine that had me pinned to the chair. I was FREE!! Yay!! Thank you!!

But then I suddenly thought, "But wait a minute... does that mean he gets to get away with it??" The Master rolled his eyes, and handed me the end of the ball of twine again!

I asked her if I could use her story in my blog. I know, it doesn't have a thing to do with bees – they don't bother about blaming and they never get tangled up in webs of their own devising the way we people do. Let's learn from the bees – and from Jill.

BeeAttitude for Day #112: *Blessed are those who forgive, for they shall fly (or walk) freely.*

One thing Fran is grateful for right now: *Linus, one of the Agriculture Department's "Beagle Brigade," whose handler brought him to Murder Goes South last Saturday for a demonstration of how he sniffs out contraband plants, fruits, and vegetables at the airport. After the show Linus gave me doggie kisses.*

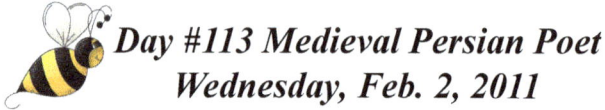 Day #113 Medieval Persian Poet
Wednesday, Feb. 2, 2011

When I was in college, I came across the translation of a poem by a medieval Persian poet. A few days ago, I came across a scrap of paper with the poem scribbled on it.

Back flooded the memories not only of the poem, but also of the circumstances under which I first found it. It was spring. I was madly in love with someone who did not know I existed. I pined over the unrequited love. I memorized poems by the dozen. Some of them I still recall even now, umpty years later.

Here's the one by a Persian:

"If of thy mortal goods thou art bereft
And from thy slender stores
Two loaves alone to thee are left,
Sell one, and with the dole
Buy hyacinths to feed thy soul."
—*Sheikh Moslih Eddin Saadi*

I decided to add some hyacinth bulbs to my plant order. My bees would like that, don't you think?

BeeAttitude for Day #113: *Blessed are the [good] poets, for their work shall endure, but why don't they write about us bees?*

One thing Fran is grateful for right now: *The crock-pot macaroni and cheese my grandson and I cooked Tuesday. Leftovers are great!*

Happy Groundhog Day

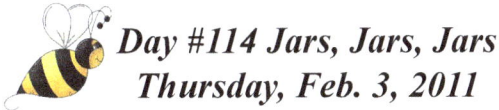 ## Day #114 Jars, Jars, Jars
Thursday, Feb. 3, 2011

Maybe I'm getting ahead of myself.

Shortly after I started this blog, my dear friend Susan Larson gave me a box full of decorative jars. "For your honey," she said.

I've spent months saying that I might not get any honey the first season. It's not good to take too much from the bees. They need enough of their stores to make it through the winter.

On one level, I know all that. But I think I've been fooling myself. What I'm *really* hoping is that my bees will be so delighted with their new home that they'll gather nectar like crazy and make enough honey for an army.

I admit it. I went and ordered a whole bunch more jars from Brushy Mountain Bee Farm. Just in case the ones from Susan wouldn't hold the entire run.

Well, they'll always keep until next year if necessary. (But I hope they won't have to.)

BeeAttitude for Day #114: *Blessed are the optimists, because they're more fun to be around than dreary old pessimists.*

One thing Fran is grateful for right now: *The new arrangement in my office. Now I can see the bird feeder better when I sit at my computer.*

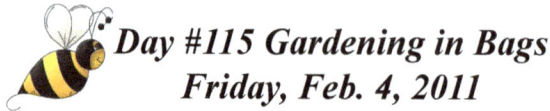 Day #115 Gardening in Bags
Friday, Feb. 4, 2011

I found a great article in Mother Earth News (the only magazine I subscribe to) about how to start a garden in bags of soil. Sounded great to me, since my "back yard" is a small strip of weedy ground between the house and the woods, strewn with spiky round seedpods *[better known as porcupine eggs]* from the sour-gum trees. The thought of trying to turn it over and delete all the weeds has kept me – well – NOT gardening back there for the past six years.

This year, all that's going to change. I've bought three bags of soil (that's all I can fit in the trunk of my little car without tipping its front tires off the road). I laid them in a row, side by side to keep weeds from growing up between them.

When the weather is right, I'll cut a big rectangle out of the top surface, poke drainage holes down through the bottom, and plant my seeds. Lettuce and beets to start with, followed by tomatoes and dill and chives, scallions and parsley and nasturtiums and marigolds. The list goes on.

Now all I have to do is buy 25 more bags. And straw to put around the ends of the bags to keep the weeds from growing up in the pathways and over the edges. Home Depot, here I come…

Boy, am I going to have a busy spring and summer.

BeeAttitude for Day #115: *Blessed are they who garden, for we shall pollinate their plants and they shall have food in abundance.*

One thing Fran is grateful for right now: *The downy woodpecker eating homemade suet outside my window as I write this.*

 Day #116 Cleaning Out Boxes of Junk
Saturday, Feb. 5, 2011

How can I possibly accumulate so much absolutely worthless detritus in one room?

Thursday afternoon I had a few hours to spend, and I tackled the boxes of stuff—yes, stuff—sitting around the sides of my office. I hate to admit it, but my usual way of dealing with pieces of paper that I don't know what to do with is to pile them in a handy cardboard box. Once that one is overflowing I set another empty box on top of it and proceed to fill it up.

The third box down had things in it from **2007**. Good grief! My enormous recycling bin is filled almost to overflowing.

But I did find a few goodies in there:
A cat toy I'd forgotten about
Some school pictures of my children (who are now grown)
Seven pretty rocks
More half-used notebooks than I can shake a stick at
A gorgeous photograph of an eagle
A gray hat I knitted a few years ago
And—here's where the bees come into this monologue—two thin sheets of beeswax designed to be rolled into candles (the package even includes the wicks).

I seem to recall having bought the candle kit originally so I could roll candles with my niece when I visited her in Colorado Springs. We tried it. They didn't burn very well, which is why I still have the makings of the last two candles. But we had fun doing it, so I guess it was worth it.

I don't think I'll go into the candle business.

BeeAttitude for Day #116: *Blessed are those who leave the beeswax for the bees, for we shall make better use of it.*

One thing Fran is grateful for right now: *movies I can watch on my computer*

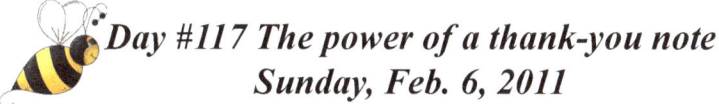 Day #117 The power of a thank-you note
Sunday, Feb. 6, 2011

A woman named Linda R emailed me out of the blue yesterday. Here's what she said:

Dear Ms. Stewart,

I wished to send a quick note so that I might express my pleasure in reading your mystery series with Biscuit the librarian (which I am) and Marmalade (I have 5). I just ordered *A Slaying Song Tonight* (even though it's not part of the series). I look forward to reading it when it arrives.

I just finished *Indigo as an Iris*. I found your *Orange as Marmalade* through a used paperback store in the town where I live. I enjoyed it because the librarian wasn't doing extraordinary things (whether extremely clever or dumb) and the cat was doing the extraordinary things. I appreciated the concept of the gratitude list - although my mother instilled the idea of being thankful of what we had at the end of the day. I do hope your Biscuit & Marmalade series will continue. I look forward to the next one.

And, I thoroughly enjoyed listening to your Mystery Matters author interviews.

Although I'm not into bees (allergic to wasp stings), I will enjoy following your blog.

Thank you again for your wonderful stories of Biscuit & Marmalade.

    Sincerely,
    Linda

What I know she didn't realize is that I've been in a carefully disguised blue funk for the past two months, wondering if I could ever possibly write another mystery, wondering if I had any stories left.

But seeing my books through her eyes, I realized that I do still want to discover the rest of the saga. So, I *will* write that next book. And the one after that. Bob will be going into beekeeping (naturally!)

Thank you, Linda. And please know that an allergy to wasp stings has nothing to do with honeybees. I wish you plenty of honey, and if you email me your address, I'll send you some of mine (as soon as I get it from the bees) as a simple indication of my deep gratitude for your kind words.

BeeAttitude for Day #117: *Blessed are those who take the time to give thanks, even though they may never know what a blessing their words are.*

One thing Fran is grateful for right now: *Linda*

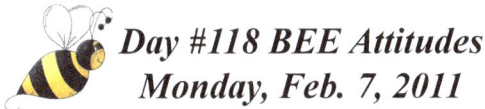 Day #118 BEE Attitudes
Monday, Feb. 7, 2011

Several people have asked me why I always include a "BeeAttitude" at the end of each blog post, so I thought I'd clear that up for everyone.

In the Biscuit McKee mysteries I write, Marmalade (the orange and white tabby cat who adopts Biscuit, the librarian) makes comments in italics here and there throughout the books, but her people simply think she's purring, so they miss out on the benefit of her wisdom.

I've tried my best to portray that cat as a *cat,* instead of as a small human with fur. I know my own cats make comments at me on a regular basis, but I'm sorry to say I generally miss the drift of their conversation. Still I think I have a reasonably good idea of the sorts of philosophic principles a feline would have.

So, when it came time to write this blog, it seemed only fair to let the bees have their say. If I've misinterpreted them, I can only hope they'll forgive me.

BeeAttitude for Day #118: *Blessed are those who help to warm the hive this time of year, for we shall let them circle to the middle to recover from their shivers.*

One thing Fran is grateful for right now: *The Aurora Theater in Lawrenceville GA, where I laughed my way through the Sunday matinee of* Sirens.

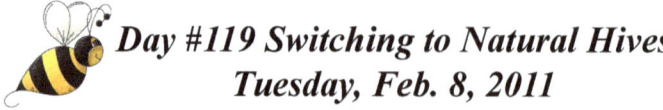
Day #119 Switching to Natural Hives
Tuesday, Feb. 8, 2011

Since the bees I'll be picking up in seven weeks (only SEVEN!) will have been raised on pre-formed foundations, and since they will have been treated with various medications, because that's what the bee farm where I'm getting them does for its bees, it's liable to take me a while to wean the bees off those conditions and into the natural set-up I want to encourage.

For "natural" beekeepers, survival of the fittest is a way of life. Hives that are not strong enough to fend off invasions of small hive beetles or varroa mites will ultimately fail. I plan to put in vegetable oil traps to help get rid of some of those pesky beetles, but what I truly want to do is raise bees with a minimum of intervention.

Keep reminding me of this, will you?

BeeAttitude for Day #119: *Blessed are they who live simply, for they shall move with a light heart from one day to the next.*

One thing Fran is grateful for right now: *My daughter with whom I can now talk "woman to woman."*

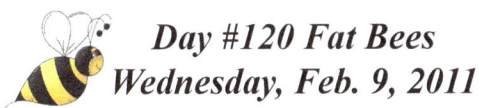 ## Day #120 Fat Bees
Wednesday, Feb. 9, 2011

Fat bees? That's not what I want.

Commercial beekeepers have created bees that are **30%** heavier than bees are meant to be. The change to large-cell foundation has forced the little bees to grow bigger, presumably so they can create more honey. But the final result has been bees that are more susceptible to diseases.

Fat bees can't easily forage in cold weather or in hot weather.
Fat bees can't dig out the bug pests that invade a hive.
Fat bees can't fly as far from the hive to gather pollen, propolis, or nectar.
Fat bees are not as healthy as the bees sized by Mother Nature, so they need to be medicated regularly by the beekeepers.

Why would anyone want to propagate fat bees, when Mother N's been telling the bees all along (for more than a hundred million years) how to stay healthy and happy?

Let's hear it for Mother Nature! And the next time you buy honey – find out about who produced it and how.

BeeAttitude for Day #120: *Blessed are they who let us live as we were intended to live, for they shall have their gardens pollinated and shall eat healthy honey.*

One thing Fran is grateful for right now: *April Myers, the managing editor of* The Pen Woman *magazine.*

Fran Stewart

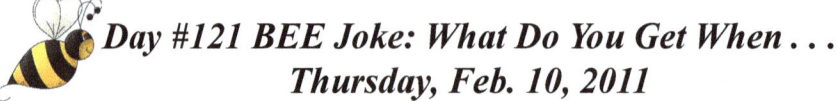

Day #121 BEE Joke: What Do You Get When . . .
Thursday, Feb. 10, 2011

I need a laugh, don't you? So . . .

What do you get when you cross a bee with a giraffe?

Either post your answers here or **email them to me.**

BEEattitude for Day # 121: *Blessed are people who like to laugh. Laughter is its own reward.*

One thing Fran is grateful for right now: *My sister*

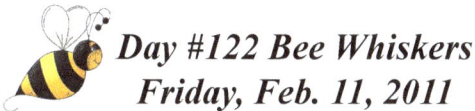 Day #122 Bee Whiskers
Friday, Feb. 11, 2011

Eight or ten years ago, I attended an elaborate Sewing Expo. Why I did it remains a mystery, since I've never been particularly interested in sewing, unlike my sister who is an amazing fabric artist. You can check out her website at depressionvisible.com to see pictures of her art pieces that show what depression feels like. She REALLY knows how to sew.

While I was at the Expo, though, bewildered by all the sewing machines and patterns, I spotted a vendor with a long table filled with implements—more kinds of scissors than I could imagine. And tweezers.

I waited for two customers to step away before I motioned to the vendor to come help me. "I'm looking for a really good pair of tweezers," I whispered across the display case. "I have this . . ." I looked around to be sure I wouldn't be overheard, ". . .this *whisker* on my chin."

"You have a whisker?" he boomed out in a strident voice that carried far past the aisle I stood on. "I have some perfect tweezers for that!" He showed me a small plastic tube containing those perfect tweezers, then handed duplicates to the dozen or so women who had descended on us within seconds, drawn there by his exceedingly loud question.

"We all have them, honey," the woman standing next to me said, as she shelled out the rather stiff purchase price to this brilliant salesman. I got in line behind six other customers.

So I was intrigued when I got to reading about the body hairs on bees. It seems that a sick bee will frequently lose all her fuzz. That's when the other bees know it's time to toss her out of the hive. See? Whiskers on females serve a purpose.

Still – hand me those marvelous tweezers. I am *not* a bee.

BeeAttitude for Day #122: *Blessed are the fuzzy, for they are soft and we like them.*

One thing Fran is grateful for right now: *Skype, so I can see my friends when I talk to them.*

Day #123 Liquid Wax, Great Big Mess
Saturday, Feb. 12, 2011

Friday I melted beeswax that I had ordered from one of the supply companies. To minimize the danger of fire, I did it over a pan of boiling water. Once it was liquid, I poured a thin bead along the top bars to give the bees a line to follow when they're building their comb.

Or, that was the idea. Do you know how messy it is trying to dribble hot wax in a thin line? I have no idea what the bees will make of the mess I created. I hope it doesn't confuse them too much, or the *honeycomb* will end up being *ohembycno*.

BeeAttitude for Day #123: *Blessed are those who try new skills, for they shall eventually succeed.*

One thing Fran is grateful for right now: *The recorded book I listened to while I struggled with the wax. It's called* <u>Captive Queen</u>, *the story of Eleanor of Aquitaine and Henry II. I'm glad I don't live in the 12th century.*

 ## *Day #124 Starting Seeds*
Sunday, Feb. 13, 2011

Don't start your seeds until Valentine's Day. That's what Brennan Washington of Phoenix Gardens told me when I took his seed-starting class.

But my grandkids were here last Monday, and the little seed-starting pellets were all lined up waiting, and the pictures on the seed packets looked so inviting. We filled 72 "pockets" in the seed tray and turned on the light above them. I should have paid attention to Brennan's instructions to group like-minded seeds together.

Public Domain Photo of Bee on Zinnia

Some of them germinate in 3 days and some of them in 10. Once the seedlings have sprouted, I'm supposed to take the plastic cover off so they can get air circulation. But here I am with a dozen infant zinnias climbing to the light (and probably suffocating in the humidity), while the other 60 seeds lie around waiting for Valentine's Day.

I'm doing this for the bees, so they'll have plenty of nectar-bearing plants to choose from. I'm doing it wrong, though. Is it too late to start over again?

BeeAttitude for Day #124: *Blessed are those who send answers to the bee jokes, for we shall get to laugh at the replies.*

One thing Fran is grateful for right now: *Lunching with my daughter.*

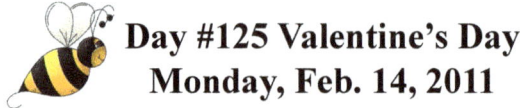 **Day #125 Valentine's Day
Monday, Feb. 14, 2011**

I Love Bees!

I'm working on my book most of the day today, and tomorrow, and the next day...

When I'm on a roll, I like to take advantage of the time, so this is a short entry.

Bee joke answers coming up tomorrow. If you haven't yet sent in your answer to:
What do you get when you cross a bee with a giraffe?
get it in before about 10:00 tonight.

BeeAttitude for Day #125: *Blessed are those who know how to love, for they shall bee loved in return.*

One thing Fran is grateful for right now: *Hot chocolate, and all the people I truly love*

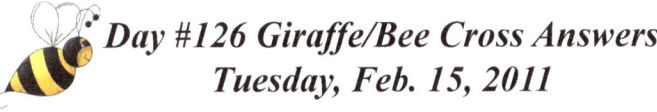 Day #126 Giraffe/Bee Cross Answers
Tuesday, Feb. 15, 2011

A few days ago, I asked *What do you get when you cross a bee with a giraffe?*

Here are the answers so far:
GA: A four-legged bee
NY: A six-legged giraffe
TX: A gibeeffe
GA: A bee-raffe
MD: A gee
FL: A winged dude wearing camouflage
IL: I don't know, but it has a very loud buzz.
SD: If the giraffe has the dominant gene for size, you'd better stay away from the tail.
NC: A black-tongued wonder
GA: Was that bee a drone or a queen? You'd get two different critters...
MS: LOTS of honey!

BeeAttitude for Day #126: *Blessed are those who let well enough alone, for they shall not end up with a mess on their hands.*

One thing Fran is grateful for right now: *Spreadsheets for keeping track of information*

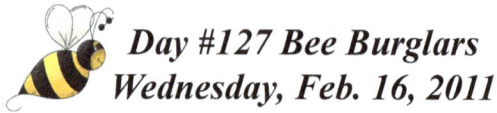

Day #127 Bee Burglars
Wednesday, Feb. 16, 2011

We've talked about the way killer bees infiltrate a hive, but what I'd like to mention today is *hive robbing* by regular little worker honeybees.

If a hive is weak—because of an inefficient queen, perhaps, or because the hive simply isn't well enough populated—then bees from other hives will do their best to sneak in and rob the honey and pollen stores. If the beekeeper is feeding with sugar water, the intruders will take that as well, leaving the original hive inhabitants to starve. I hope this is something I never have to deal with.

How to avoid a problem? I'm glad you asked. There are four possibilities:

Monitor the hive to catch problems before they get serious. That's what the books say, as if I'm supposed to know what to look for.

Feed the bees at the rear of the hive rather than right at the front door, so that robbers would have to negotiate the length of the hive and would probably be stopped before they got to their goal. Langstroth hives are traditionally built to accommodate an entrance feeder. This makes it harder for the guard bees to keep out a mass of intruders. The beehives I'm buying (and the ones I'll build) all feed at the rear, however, so I should be okay.

Reduce the size of the entrance. You can buy fancy entrance reducers, but my hives have a small hole as the entrance to begin with. That's the usual design of top bar hives as well, so when I build mine, I'll put in three entrance holes and cork the ones that aren't ready to be used yet. (I'll explain this in a later blog.)

As a last resort, break up a weak hive by eliminating the queen and placing that hive's brood comb in a stronger hive. I've said it before: I DON'T want to squish a queen, so this last resort will probably never be used at BeesKnees Beekeeping.

And now, while we're talking about burglars, here's a fun story from a National Public Radio blog. *[2019 Note: the original NPR video has been taken down, but I found it again on YouTube]* https://www.youtube.com/watch?v=fDX7tevXO1E. If this link doesn't work, just Google Dusty the Cat Burglar.

BeeAttitude for Day #127: *Blessed are those who keep their feet to themselves, for we shall not resort to stinging them.*

One thing Fran is grateful for right now: *Steve Reiman, founder of Therapy Dogs of Vermont, who sent me the original NPR blog link*

 ## *Day #128 Captain Jack Sparrow*
Thursday, Feb. 17, 2011

I'm not sure what bees think of cats, or what cats think of bees, but you can't have read this blog or any of my writings for very long without knowing that I'm one of those cat people. *Crazy lady with cats*, some might say. I have two grand-dogs I love, but for sheer day-to-day companionship, I prefer the feline variety.

When I look out my office window, I can see the resting places of a number of my dear old furry friends. Some of them were relatively young when they died of various ailments; some of them had gotten on in cat years. There comes a time when they have to go, and while I firmly believe that there is a reason, a soul-based reason, for every death, it still isn't any easier when that time comes, particularly since our animal companions don't always let us know it's their time to go.

Sparrow in the Sink © 2010 by Petie Ogg

Yesterday, Petie Ogg emailed me from Texas to say that the final time had come unexpectedly for their dear sweet Captain Jack Sparrow. I'm so sorry for your loss, Petie. We've become friends through this blog, and even though I never met Jack, I know his love must have enriched the lives of your family.

When animals die, they cross the Rainbow Bridge to a beautiful land where they live happily together. Often, though, one of them will perk up its ears and trot happily back to the end of the Rainbow Bridge to greet a long-loved person who is finally making the same trip. I feel sure that my dear old friends will be there to greet me when it's my turn to cross that bridge, and I'm equally sure that Jack will wait for you, Petie.

BeeAttitude for Day #128: *Blessed are they who love animals, for we animals shall, each in our own way, love them in return.*

One thing Fran is grateful for right now: *The irises that grow above the graves of Waldo and Jazzminka*

Day #129 I did it!
Friday, Feb. 18, 2011

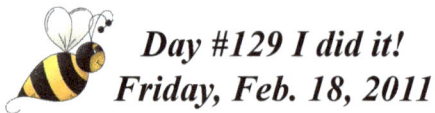

You may recall that I've had some trepidation about lighting my smoker. In fact, I've tried several times (times I didn't admit to in this blog) and failed miserably.

But Thursday afternoon I dug the slightly charred remains of my last attempts from the guts of the smoker and started anew out on the back deck.

1. Tear off some strips of newspaper. Stuff them in the smoker.

2. Gather your fuel (in my case, pine needles) and stow them nearby.
3. Tear another strip of newspaper (seven or eight sheets thick) and light one end.
4. Try not to incinerate your hand as you stuff the burning paper into the smoker.
5. Give it a few gallant wheezes with the attached bellows, enough to send clouds of smoke into the air.
6. Finish coughing and move upwind from the contraption.
7. Now stuff your fuel in on top of the burning paper.
8. Close the lid.
9. Pump the bellows like crazy and watch the smoke billow forth.

This time I got it to stay smoking for twenty minutes! That should be long enough to check my hives, right? I hope my bees turn out to be patient with me.

BeeAttitude for Day #129: *Blessed are those who practice their skills <u>before</u> they need them, for they shall be prepared when the time comes.*

One thing Fran is grateful for right now: *The Maté-dor Chai tea I bought at Aris**tea**crats in Lawrenceville. It's so tasty, I decided to mention it in my next book.*

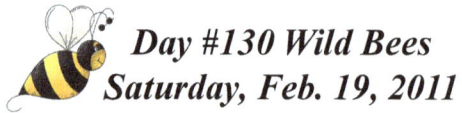
Day #130 Wild Bees
Saturday, Feb. 19, 2011

Last week we had one of those gorgeous sunny afternoons that tempted me away from my writing. I threw on a jacket and headed out to the creek that runs through my back yard.

While I stood on the bank, I glanced up the hill on the opposite bank, through the tangle of discarded branches and stumps from the (former) trees my neighbor had cut down five years ago. Lo and behold, above one vine-entwined thicket I saw a cloud of bees, careening ecstatically around the stump, apparently on one of those cleansing flights that bees engage in as soon as a warmish day turns up after a winter of confinement in their hives.

If I'd been a Neanderthal, I would have seen that bee-cloud as a harbinger of sweets, and I would have gone after it with my bare hands.

I'm happy indeed that I'll be able to gather honey from a civilized box on my back deck, having first puffed smoke into the hive to calm the bees, instead of trying to fight my way through the brambles to tear open a fallen log.

I would have made a lousy Neanderthal.

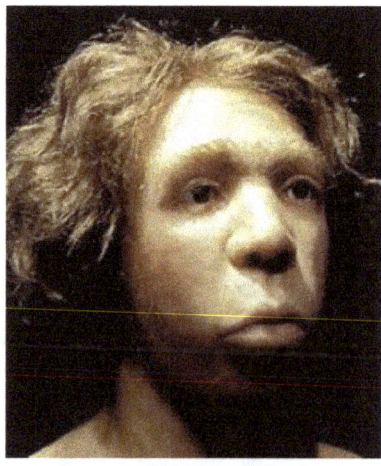
© Wikipedia

BeesKnees #2: A Beekeeping Memoir

BeeAttitude for Day #130: *Blessed are they who keep our hives intact, for we shall remain in one place instead of swarming away.*

One thing Fran is grateful for right now: *The daffodils beginning to poke their way up through the leaves*

 Day #131 The Garden is Getting Ready
Sunday, Feb. 20, 2011

Remember those beet seeds I planted WAY too early almost a month ago? They've started to come up. Now I have to worry about the weather.

And the sweet peas, zinnia, portulaca, and dill my grandkids sowed in the seed-starter pots? They're up, too, straining to overgrow the grow-light I have above them. Too early to put them outside. Running out of room in my office, where they're perched on the top of a long filing cabinet.

Yikes! What do I do?

Photo Credit: Pexels.com

Bees are smart. They wait until the weather is exactly right. Of course, if these early plants make it, I'll have beets and flowers and herbs ready to pick in no time at all.

I think I like the suspense! And the fact that I won't have to wonder if the dandelions will survive. Of course they will.

BeeAttitude for Day #131: *Blessed are those who plant, for they shall reap the benefits.*
And blessed are those who let the weeds grow, for they shall reap benefits as well.

One thing Fran is grateful for right now: *The full moon last night*

Day #132 When am I going to stain my deck?
Monday, Feb. 21, 2011

I hadn't thought about this particular wrinkle in my beekeeping to-do list.

I stain my deck every few years to protect the wood. The stain is supposed to be applied when the weather is relatively warm. The trouble is, when it gets warm enough to stain the deck, I'll be picking up my bees and installing them—yep—on the deck.

The last thing I want is for them to get stuck in the wet stain. Of course, I don't want my deck to rot away, either. Will you keep your fingers crossed for a spell of warm-enough weather the week *before* the bees are ready?

I need all the luck I can get on this one.

BeeAttitude for Day #132: *Blessed are those who do preventive maintenance, for they shall have less to worry about.*

One thing Fran is grateful for right now: *Potting soil*

Day #133 Branding
Tuesday, Feb. 22, 2011

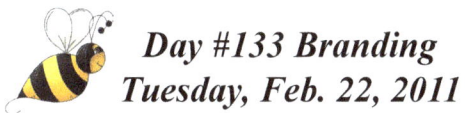

With a title like "Branding," you probably thought I was going to talk about marketing, right? Isn't everyone into branding nowadays – making sure their public image is packaged tidily?

Forget it. I'm talking about real BRANDING. My branding iron arrived yesterday.

No! I'm not going to apply a **hot branding iron** to my bees!

But I *am* going to brand the hives. It all came about when I was reading one of those dire doom-and-gloom articles about people who steal hives. Lousy thought. Of course, the large commercial outfits are much more likely to see thieves lurking about than the teeny back-yard beekeepers, so I didn't really *have* to mark my hives.

And I certainly didn't want to use magic markers to write PROPERTY OF FRAN STEWART. IF FOUND PLEASE RETURN TO . . . Ugly, ugly.

So, I checked out https://www.brandnew.net I found them because their advertisement has shown up several times in the ad column to the left of this blog. I noted the URL and went to their website.

I sent them a rather stark design that showed what I wanted, bemoaning the fact that I didn't know how to put a bee in the middle of it. Lo and behold, a very nice person emailed me back and said he could put a bee in there.

Within the next week or so, my son's going to drive out here with his propane torch (to heat the iron), and after he leaves, each one of my hive boxes will sport the following logo (but you'll have to imagine the cute little bee in between the two lines, since I can't figure out how to reproduce it):

Fran Stewart

Bees Knees
Bee logo here
Beekeeping

Now I get to join that illustrious list of BrandNew customers . . .

The White House
Ghiradelli Chocolate
Mayo Clinic
Disney World, and
BeesKnees . . . !

BeeAttitude for Day #133: *Blessed are the businesses that give good value, for they shall receive accolades from their clients.*

One thing Fran is grateful for right now: *The possum who cleans up the excess birdseed that falls under my porch*

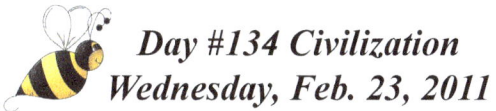
Day #134 Civilization
Wednesday, Feb. 23, 2011

I keep saying in this blog that bees haven't really changed since their beginnings. Well, guess what? I'm not too sure people have changed much either. We have increased our technology and our languages. But have we changed in any substantive way? Are human beings any different than they were a couple of million years ago?

I once was asked in a class to explain how people have changed over the course of history. My answer, I'm sorry to say, was that as people became more "civilized," they simply increased the distance over which they could hurt each other.

Think about it. A bee butts a person to scare him away from the hive. As a last resort, the bee will sting, thereby killing herself. This has been true for more than 140 million years. Now think about people. We, like bees, used to be able to hurt people only if they were close by, within an arm's length of us. Then, with such tools as language and weapons, we gradually extended the range over which we could cause pain.

On the other hand, we've also increased the distance at which we can cause joy. A phone call from my sister or a dear friend can brighten my day considerably, no matter how far that person is from me geographically. A well-written book brings me joy even if the author is on the far side of the county—or the globe—or on the far side of the grave.

Bees still have to "bee" right next to each other to communicate, but we humans can reach each other happily at any distance. What a relief. Maybe there's hope for us humans after all.

BeeAttitude for Day #134: *Blessed are the children, for they shall be the harvesters of tomorrow.*

One thing Fran is grateful for right now: *My dear friend Lyn, who knows about "Human Design"*

Day #135 Writers Boot Camp
Thursday, Feb. 24, 2011

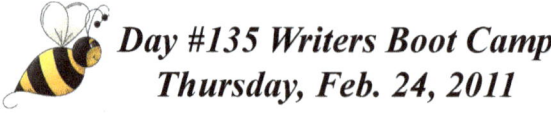

What fun! I spent time yesterday speaking to fifth-grade students at Woodward Mill Elementary School as part of their *Writer's Boot Camp* program. The topic was **"Draw Your Reader into Your Story: Pick the Right Verb."**

We talked about how changing the verbs can change the whole intent of the story. For instance, we started one story this way:
Mom **pulled** to a stop beside the road.
Then we wrote the same story, changing nothing but the verbs, and it started like this:
Mom **screeched** to a stop beside the road.
Two different verbs. Two different scenarios. See?

At the board, I wrote, "The lion _____ across the grassland."
We quickly discarded tired words like *ran* or *walked*. Instead, they supplied fifteen or twenty vivid verbs, including:

- limped
- staggered
- stalked
- bounded
- crept
- roared

In "I _____ the picture from my grandfather," they suggested verbs such as:

- adored
- burned
- destroyed
- inherited
- detested
- evaluated

Eventually I'd like to get an observation hive so I can haul it to the school and introduce them to the joys of raising bees—just as much fun and just as important as the joys of writing effectively.

BeeAttitude for Day #135: *Blessed are the teachers, for they shall be illuminated by the light of knowledge.*

Something Fran is grateful for right now: *The students who jumped in joyfully with answers*

Fran Stewart

Day #136 Bees Don't Have to Apologize
Friday, Feb. 25, 2011

People who make lists and schedules are optimists, because they have the underlying belief that they'll be able to check off each one of those items and make each one of those appointments.

That usually works around this house, except when the computer acts up. Writing used to be done with a pencil or a clickety old typewriter, and while I still do a lot of drafts longhand, ultimately the 'puter must be warmed up.

I write each of these blog entries the day *before*, so I can post them just after midnight, EDT. Guess what happened last night? Penelope Puter wouldn't cooperate. That maddening little blue circle kept twining its way around the screen, no matter what I tried to click on.

At least the power button still worked, so I finally shut the whole thing down. Of course, this morning, Penelope informed me, rather sternly, that this was all my fault, since I had not powered her off properly and she was going to have to spin her wheels for quite some time trying to make sure my stupid actions hadn't caused egregious errors in my documents.

Okay, so maybe she didn't use exactly those words, but the whiney tone was definitely present. Whatever happened to the concept of an apology?

I'm terribly sorry, Miss Frannie, that my internal workings screwed up royally yesterday, causing you to miss a deadline or two. It was all my fault, and I hope you can find it in your heart to forgive me. I'll try to do a better job in the future.
  Your friend,
  Penelope Puter

Bees never have these kinds of problems.

BeeAttitude for Day #136: *Blessed are those who apologize nicely when they err, for they shall be appreciated.*

One thing Fran is grateful for right now: *Singing, even if I'm a bit glum. Especially when I'm a bit glum.*

Day #137 Nightmares and Common Sense
Saturday, Feb. 26, 2011

I dreamed last night that a bear wandered up from the creek and ripped open my beehives to steal the honey. Yikes! I don't even have the bees yet. What'll I do when they're actually installed on my back deck?

Of course, I've never yet seen a bear paw print (much less a bear) on the creek bank, just some raccoons and possums, so I probably won't ever have to worry about Winnie-the-Pooh's cousins.

Worry is the interest you pay on a loan you've never taken out, so I guess I should just forget the bad dreams and sleep easier. Good idea.

BeeAttitude for Day #137: *Blessed are the calm of mind, for they shall take their rest with ease.*

One thing Fran is grateful for right now: Cowans Book Nook *in Blue Ridge GA, where I'll be signing books today (Saturday) from noon to three.* [*2019 Note:* Cowan's Book Nook went out of business several years after this. At one of my book launches there, a woman came into the store, spoke with the owner for quite a while, wrote down the names of several of the books the owner had suggested, and then said, "I can get them cheaper on Amazon." And we wonder why so many bookstores have gone out of business.]

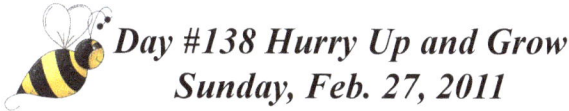
Day #138 Hurry Up and Grow
Sunday, Feb. 27, 2011

Well, my Kentucky Wonder beans have not only sprouted, but they're threatening to take over my office. The tomato plants are huge, the potatoes are growing faster than I can mound the dirt up around them, and the sweet pea vines are beginning to twine around each other. Help! Spring needs to get here faster so I can get these babies outside!

I just hope I have things blooming by the time the bees are installed (four weeks to go...). I'd hate to have to feed them too much sugar water. Maybe I should start the bees out <u>inside</u> my house—I have plenty of plants in here so far.

Wouldn't the cats love having all those flying buddies?

Q: What do you get when you cross a cat with a bee?
A: One *very* cross cat

BeeAttitude for Day #138: *Blessed are those who plant flowers, for we shall pollinate their gardens with gusto.*

One thing Fran is grateful for right now: *The customers at Cowan's Book Nook in Blue Ridge yesterday when I was there signing my books*

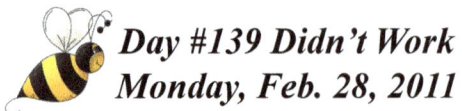 ### *Day #139 Didn't Work*
Monday, Feb. 28, 2011

My son, Eli, had told me he'd stop by Sunday afternoon with a propane torch so we could brand the bee hives (see my blog for Feb. 22nd), but then he ended up doing something else much more fun—building sixteen pairs of stilts.

This is what my branding iron looks like.

I didn't want to wait, though, so on the **warmest** day of Spring so far, I built a fire in the fireplace and waited for a nice bed of coals. While the wood was burning down, I hauled the hive boxes out onto the deck and lined them up so I'd be sure and get the brand right side up instead of upside down.

Once the fire was settled in, I stuck the brand in the coals and let it sit there long enough to get really hot. Brand in hand, feeling very cowboy-ish, I strode to the deck and planted the branding iron on the first box.

It didn't work. It wasn't the fault of brandnew.net. They told me to use a propane torch. They are not responsible for my impatience.

I put the branding iron back in the coals and tried again. And again. And again. Then I gave up. I'll wait for my son and the propane torch. Four weeks to go till the bees will be ready, so there's plenty of time. Meanwhile, I've opened all the windows to let out the heat from the fireplace.

BeeAttitude for Day #139: *Blessed are those who try, for (sometimes) they shall succeed*

One thing Fran is grateful for right now: *The squirrels who've cleaned*

up the suet that melted onto the rocks beneath the feeder.
I tried to make my own suet.
It, like the branding, didn't work.
I'm headed to Wild Birds Unlimited to buy some.

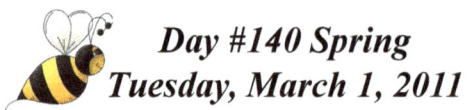

Day #140 Spring
Tuesday, March 1, 2011

I just need to see a bunch of flowers, don't you? Yesterday there were so many thunderstorms in the evening I began to feel like a target. Luckily, all the trees around my house are still intact, although one LARGE branch ended up in my driveway (no idea where it came from).

I'd hate to be a bee in this weather, with those teeny little wings, up against the buffetings of Mother Nature. It would be more fun to be a bee in the sunshine on a flower.

I wish I'd thought to go out on the deck during the storm to see what the wind gusts felt like on the side where I'll be putting the hives. I wonder how many bricks it takes to weight down the covers so they won't blow off in a storm?

BeeAttitude for Day #140: *Blessed are those who look up at the sky, for they shall see wonders indeed.*

One thing Fran is grateful for right now: *The sausage tetrazzini I made for dinner Friday (and the leftovers on Saturday and Sunday)*

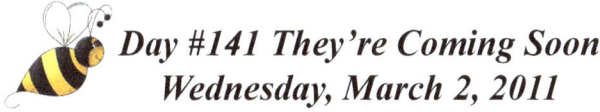 Day #141 They're Coming Soon
Wednesday, March 2, 2011

When I started this blog last October, it seemed like the bees were a distant goal. I'm glad I've spent this much time getting ready for them. I'm also really, really glad that they won't need me to be perfect. Heck, bees have been around longer than people—longer than the dinosaurs, in fact—and they're good at what they do.

I figure they'll be rather like honored house guests, ones who will mind their manners and leave a gift of honey every so often.

Four weeks or so . . . and I still don't know how to get the pictures out of my phone and onto my computer. I think I need a thirty-dollar doohickey. Anybody know where a doohickey store is?

BeeAttitude for Day #141: *Blessed are those who plan ahead, for their surprises shall be elegant indeed. Frannie truly has no idea just what we bees are going to bring to her life.*

One thing Fran is grateful for right now: *The woodpecker and the male cardinal sitting peacefully on my bird feeder as I write this.*

Day #142 Don't go to a gardening center
Thursday, March 3, 2011

Why did I say "*DON'T* go to a gardening center" as the title to this blog?

Because I just did go to such a place. And I ended up blowing my budget. But then I had the fun of coming home and planting creeping thymes and hellebores and a gorgeous rosemary bush. The biggest rosemary bush I've ever seen was at the last house I owned, and I've missed it (the bush, not the house) ever since. I planted the one today right over where Rimski is buried.

Here's what Rimski looked like when he was a kitten:

© Yelloideas Photography

Then he got bigger and lounged around on the computer monitor in my son's house. When my son had to go overseas, his cats came to live with me. And I didn't give them back.

©Yelloideas Photography

But, I've gotten off the track here. I'm so glad I've had a compost pile percolating for several years. Now that I'm finally interested in planting again (all because the bees are going to need nectar to gather), the compost is coming in handy. The only problem with using compost is that I spend a lot of time **rescuing earthworms** before I can plant anything; but then again, what else is a lovely day for if not to encourage us to take time to move deliberately and enjoy every moment?

BeeAttitude for Day #142: *Blessed are those who start plants early, for we bees shall be grateful to them.*

One thing Fran is grateful for right now: *Those earthworms*

 ## Day #143 March Forth on March Fourth
Friday, March 4, 2011

This is my absolutely favorite date of the year, every year. The day tells us to be bold, to follow our dreams, to bypass disappointments, to claim responsibility for our own actions. In short, it tells us to:

March Forth !

Good advice, isn't it? And from a calendar, no less . . .

BeeAttitude for Day #143: *Blessed are those who march forth, for they shall not be left behind.*

One thing Fran is grateful for right now: *My 7th grade English teacher, who first told me about this date.*

Day #144 The Complete Canon
Saturday, March 5, 2011

Becoming a beekeeper has been a long process – and I don't even have my bees yet. For some reason, this process reminds me a bit of the adventure that the **Atlanta Shakespeare Company** has been going through at the Shakespeare Tavern.

As of this month, they will become the third acting company in the world ever to have completed the entire canon – every play Shakespeare ever wrote. March 11th they'll open *Two Noble Kinsmen*, the story of two men who are best friends, but who fall in love with the same woman. Running in repertory on alternate evenings will be *Edward III*, which opens on March 17th. The two plays will close on April 16th and April 17th.

[2019 Note: In June of this year, the ASC completed the entire canon <u>for the second time</u>!]

Completing the canon has been a long-time dream of the ASC's artistic director, Jeffrey Watkins. I've been fortunate to serve as a volunteer at the Tavern ever since I first moved to Georgia in 1993, and I've watched the dream become a reality.

The ASC gets most of its revenue through ticket sales, so – if you've never seen a play there (or if you'd like to see another one) – head to https://www.shakespearetavern.com.

After TNK and E3 open, the Atlanta Shakespeare Company will join the rarified company of those two other acting groups who have performed every play of Shakespeare's.
- One of them (of course) is the Royal Shakespeare Academy in England.
- The other was Willie's very own acting company – the one for which he wrote all those plays.

Once I've seen both these plays, I'll join a select group of people who have, over the years, attended every single play by W.S.

And then, in early April, I'll join that select group of folks who live with bees in their backyard. **I'm looking forward to both experiences.**

BeeAttitude for Day #144: *Blessed are those who act, for their dedication shall brighten the world.*

One thing Fran is grateful for right now: *The Shakespeare Tavern and all their company of actors.*

Day #145 Bartow County Library System
Sunday, March 6, 2011

I can't just sit around here at home every day, writing my mysteries and planning for the bees. Once in a while I have to drive to a library to meet folks. That's what I did yesterday. Colleen Knight, from the Bartow County Library System, invited me (and a dozen other area writers) to a "Meet the Authors" afternoon.

NPR's "Car Talk" kept me laughing on my drive up there. I avoided the wreck on I-75 (and the resulting standstill traffic) by getting off at an earlier exit and winding through some gorgeous countryside.

There were plenty of nice people to talk to at the event. Writers really appreciate readers, and I love hearing the stories people tell of how books have influenced their lives.

I drove home safely, even though there was a pounding rainstorm all the way.

All in all a satisfying jaunt. Maybe by next year I'll have an observation hive I can take along with me. Did I mention that Biscuit's husband Bob is going to start beekeeping in my next mystery?

BeeAttitude for Day #145: *Blessed are the librarians, for they keep the light burning for future generations.*

What Fran is grateful for right now: *The people who stopped to talk, and those who bought books, too.*

 ## Day #146 Thoughts on Immortality
Monday, March 7, 2011

My thoughts have been all over the road map recently. Miss Polly, my 14-year-old cat, woke me as usual the other morning, and I got to thinking about mortality—hers and my own.

People, and cats too, live as individuals. When we see a friend walking down the street, we don't say, "Oh, there goes another member of my part of the human race." No, we call that person by name and recognize her individuality. Ditto with cats, friendly dogs, even the possum who cleans up around the bottom of my bird feeder and turns on my motion-sensor light each night.

Honeybees, on the other hand, live their short lives (six weeks for a worker bee) as simply a part of a larger unit, the hive – the way individual cells in our body do their work for a short time and then die off, to be replaced by new ones.

Eventually, our human cells—all of them—run out of gas, and we die. But think about a hive. There could conceivably be a hive somewhere in the world that is still making honey after, say, a thousand years of being in that same place. Or maybe a million or two. As the hive population grows too large, half the bees take off somewhere else (that's called "swarming"), but the other half stays behind and builds up their numbers and their honey and pollen stores all over again.

Isn't this a kind of immortality? I'd like to think it is. You see, when I'm no longer around, my bees will be able to keep going without me. They may move to a new location, but they'll still be the hive that grew and flourished on my back deck.

Come to think of it, as long as my books last, my first cat is immortalized, because she served as the model for "Marmalade."

BeeAttitude for Day #146: *Blessed are those who take good care of themselves, for they shall live long and prosper.*

One thing Fran is grateful for right now: *Romeo and Juliet, which I saw last night at the Shakespeare Tavern in Atlanta with my granddaughter. Four hundred years, and the story is still fresh. Hey! That's immortality, too, isn't it?*

p.s. It's official: this is "National Read an eBook Week."
Maybe you'd like to try my *Biscuit McKee Mysteries*.

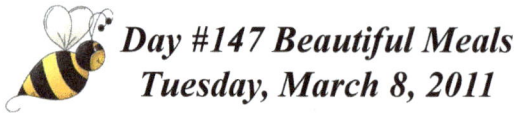 Day #147 Beautiful Meals
Tuesday, March 8, 2011

I had to share this photo with you. My son has been a vegetarian for almost 20 years. He even managed to eat a vegetarian diet when he was in the Marine Corps. I had wondered if his decision to become a vegetarian in high school was just a fad, but he's carried through with it from a deep conviction that it is the right way to eat. In the last year or two he's been eating only raw foods. Naturally, he hangs out with a lot of other people of like mind.

When he first told me about raw foods, all I could think of was carrots and celery, and a few other choice goodies. But he's convinced me that eating raw whole organic food can be an adventure - a beautiful one.

Yelloideas Photography © 2011

On his Facebook page a couple of days ago, he posted this picture, from a meal that he had shared with a group of his friends. I'm not sure who to credit with the beauty of the place setting and the gorgeous textures of the food—I'm sure it was as yummy as it looks. One of the Facebook comments said thank you to Melissa for opening her lovely home, so I would assume she created the meal. If not her, then SOMEBODY put a great deal of love and effort into these edible creations.

Thank you, Eli, for letting me use so many of your wonderful photos in my blog. They brighten it up considerably.

Now, about this photo: if only there were a little pot of natural honey in there somewhere . . .

BeeAttitude for Day #147: *Blessed are those who care about what they eat, for they shall thrive.*

One thing Fran is grateful for right now: *My printer that is so dependable*

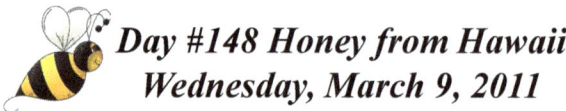 Day #148 Honey from Hawaii
Wednesday, March 9, 2011

A few days ago I received a package of pure gold. Golden honey, that is, from Hawaii. And there's a story behind it.

When I was in 11th grade, my dad was stationed at Wright-Patterson Field, and I attended Fairborn High School. I was the only junior in a senior English class, and was befriended by two girls. Over the years I've lost contact with one of them, but Ellen and I have written occasionally. When my books were published, Ellen was quite encouraging, and when I started this blog, she signed up as a follower right away.

She gardens, although—when we were both in high school—I would have been surprised to think of her in a garden. Ellen, you see, had allergies back then. One day she shuffled into English class, thoroughly miserable, with her eyes puffy and her nose sniffly. Just as class was starting she slipped me a note, a poem she'd written. Even after all these years, I recall her momentous verse:

> As far as springtime flowers go,
> They are quite beautiful, I know,
> But since I have to sneeze and sniff
> Every time I take a whiff,
> Somehow their beauty doth decrease
> With each and every little SNEECE!

Anyway, she must have recovered from her allergies. Or maybe living in Arizona makes her less susceptible. At any rate, she tasted macadamia nut honey when she and her husband visited his sister on her macadamia plantation in Hawaii four years ago. Ellen decided I hadn't lived until I'd tasted honey from macadamia trees, and she ordered a sample set from Big Island Bees.

© Big Island Bees

Three honeys, packaged in pretty jars, now grace my table. It's amazing how different they taste. Wilelaiki Honey (from the Wilelaiki tree, of course) is more spicy than sweet. The dark, rich honey from the macadamia nut blossoms tastes sort of, well, nutty. And the honey from Ohi'a Lehua blossoms isn't golden; it's a creamy white, for the honey begins to crystallize almost immediately after it is gathered. Maybe that's because the Ohi'a tree is the first to grow out of a lava flow.

As I taste-tested these delightful gifts, I couldn't help but think about how people are a lot like honey – some are spicy, some are frankly nutty, and some go through hard times and bounce right back.

BeeAttitude for Day #148: *Blessed are those who leave us enough honey when they take some of our stores, for then we bees shall thrive to make more honey.*

What Fran is grateful for right now: *Friendships that last through the years*

Day #149 The Prayer of the Children
Thursday, March 10, 2011

On Sunday I'll be singing at Spivey Hall with The Gwinnett Choral Guild. I hope you can come to the 4:00 performance. The theme will be *feeding the hungry*, and that means the hunger of the heart as well as of the belly.

One of the songs we're performing is Bestor's "The Prayer of the Children," which he wrote after having visited a war-torn land.

[2019 Note: The link in the original post was for a performance by the Baylor Men's Choir, but that was removed from their website. I found this one, performed by a group called The Gondwana Singers, a choral group for 14- to 16-year-olds—and that makes even more sense.]

Bees are smarter than humans. Even the Africanized bees, which I wrote about on Day #67 (December 17th), take over a colony fairly peacefully. Pretty much the only one who dies is the queen, after which the invader bees install their own queen and become part of the hive. **All the baby bees are safe through the whole process.**

Spivey Hall is on the campus of Clayton State College in Morrow, GA. I hope you can attend the 4:00 performance and enjoy our glorious music. If you can't be there, will you send my throat some good vibes?

BeeAttitude for Day #149: *Blessed are the peacemakers, for their hives shall grow many happy baby bees.*

Someone Fran is grateful for right now: *Composers*

Day #150 Big Island Bees in Hawaii
Friday, March 11, 2011

I went to Big Island Bees and found this information. I blatantly cut and pasted it, so if you tell anybody about how amazing bees are and use these statistics to prove it, be sure you give Big Island Honey the credit:

Each 9.5 oz. jar of Big Island Bees honey is the result of:
683 bees
flying 32,550 miles
to visit 1,185,000 flowers
to collect 5.93 lbs. of nectar.
That's a lot of work. But, it is so worth it!

Thank you, Big Island Bees. I'm still enjoying your honey on fresh biscuits for breakfast.

BeeAttitude for Day #149: *Blessed are people who appreciate bees, for they shall find honey in abundance.*

One thing Fran is grateful for right now: *The Gwinnett County Extension Service (see tomorrow's blog to find out why).*

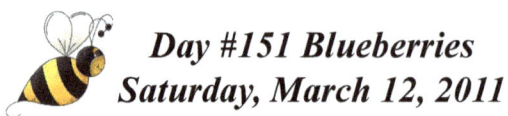

Day #151 Blueberries
Saturday, March 12, 2011

In January I ordered six blueberry plants from the extension service. Their flyer said that the pickup date would be March 10th. That sounded like a very long time to go, so I didn't bother trying to figure out where I was going to plant them.

All of a sudden, it was MARCH! So I walked my yard and tried to visualize 8' tall bushes, each of them 4' wide. I found room for five of them. Fortunately, I have a dear friend whose birthday is today. She has a lonely blueberry bush in her yard, so I asked her if she wanted another one. She said yes.

The pickup place was at the Gwinnett County Fairgrounds, and once I found the right entrance, the process was so well organized. They had dozens of volunteers to gather the plants and help load them into the cars. I'd brought some heavy cardboard boxes along with me. The bushes were anywhere from two to four feet tall. I was very glad the stems were flexible enough for me to fit them in the back seat. Sometimes I miss my old truck.

It's rained several times over the last few days, so the ground was ready for new plants. And, of course, my compost pile had plenty of good earth that I could mix in with the dirt from the five holes. I managed to get my knees thoroughly muddy, and my fingernails had enough dirt under them to start a whole package of seeds in. I love dirt!

[2019 Note: Those blueberry bushes are still going strong. I very seldom get to eat the blueberries myself, though, since the birds know exactly the right moment to snatch them from the bushes.]

BeeAttitude for Day #151: *Blessed are the people who fill their yards with plants we bees love, for they shall have gloriously healthy flora.*

What Fran is grateful for right now: *Darlene*

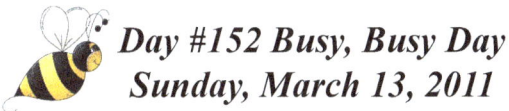 Day #152 Busy, Busy Day
Sunday, March 13, 2011

What a fun and busy day I had yesterday! My grandson's team won their soccer game. It was his very first soccer game – glad I could see it. He was having such a good time, he danced around the field, and then made a really good save while he was playing goalie.

When I got home, I spent a number of hours staining my deck (I do that every two years) because I wanted to get it done before I pick up the bees in three more weeks. Only got half of it done, and only one coat on that, but I'll keep plugging away at it.

Then, in the afternoon, Rob Alexander, one of the co-leaders of the Gwinnett Beekeepers Club, hosted all the club members at his place so we could watch as he opened and examined three of his hives. We all brought our veils and smokers for hands-on experience in how to put the blinkin' veils on in the first place *(where are these long cords supposed to go?)* and how to light the smoker.

Then came the really fun part – the bees. Lots of bees. Thousands of bees.

Part of the job of a beekeeper is to examine the hives as soon as the weather warms up in the spring, to make sure the queen is actively laying eggs and the worker bees are finding nectar. Rob's hives were quite healthy, I'm happy to report. One was even at the point where the bees were getting overcrowded, so he put on an extra hive body (he set an empty hive box on top of the full one so the queen would have more room to lay her eggs in).

He gave those of us who wanted to, a chance to pull out an active frame. My gosh, it was heavy with all that honey and all those bees. I couldn't get my bifocals working well enough to see the eggs (they're teeny white rice-like wiggles). Apparently the ones I've been looking at in books are magnified. But I DID see some of the larvae all curled up in their little cells looking like fat little C's. **C for cute!**

Here's an egg:

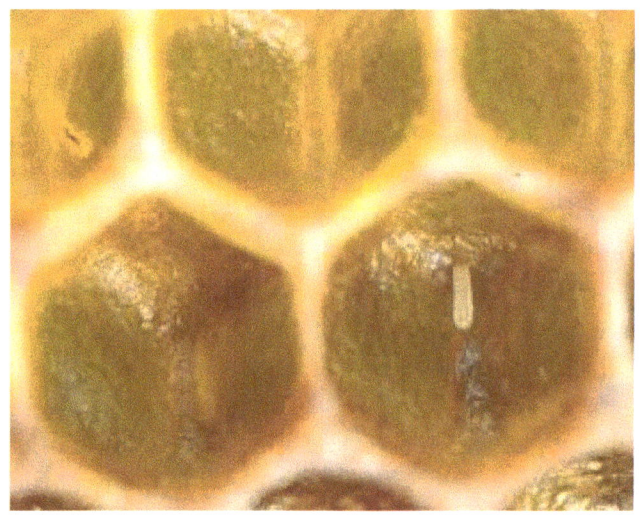

© Extension.UGA.edu

We spent such a long time asking questions and poking around the hives, the bees in the third hive got a bit perturbed with us. Rob ended up being stung four or five times—and one of those times I had to scrape the stinger out of his thumb, since he was holding a frame and didn't want to take the time to set it down. The faster you get the stinger out, the better.

We all benefited greatly from the experience, and I for one feel even better about my decision to keep bees.

BeeAttitude for Day #152: *Blessed are those who help others to learn, for they are useful indeed.*

One thing Fran is grateful for right now: *The New Dawn Theater in Duluth, where I saw a fun presentation of* Pride and Prejudice *last night.* ***I TOLD you I had a busy day!***

Day #153 Taking the time to say thank-you
Monday, March 14, 2011

Sunday afternoon the Gwinnett Choral Guild performed at Spivey Hall. What a glorious place to perform. No wonder that hall is a favorite of world-class musicians.

At any rate, after the performance was over, I wandered out through the lobby, heading toward my car. I was stopped, though, by two women who took the time to add their personal thank-you for the performance. They mentioned specific things that had brought them joy, such as the power of the *Gospel Magnificat*—and said that they'd both cried when we sang the hauntingly poignant *Prayer of the Children*.

It was so thoughtful of them to hang around for a while waiting for us to appear from the back, just so they could give more than the applause we'd received in the hall.

I've decided that for the coming week, I'm going to go out of my way, at least once each day, to say *thank you*. Won't you join me in that endeavor?

I wonder if bees have a way to say thanks? Surely, when a forager bee unloads her pollen and hands off her nectar to one of the house bees, the bee on the receiving end must wiggle her thanks one way or another. How else could bees have functioned so well for 140 million years?

BeeAttitude for Day #153: *Blessed are the music-makers, for they shall feel a deep and abiding connection with each other.*

One thing Fran is grateful for right now: *The audio book (*The Physick Book of Deliverance Dane*) that kept me company on the long trip to and from Spivey Hall. It's a great story that weaves the lives of women from Salem Massachusetts in 1692 (witch trial times) with the life of a young graduate student in the 1990s.*

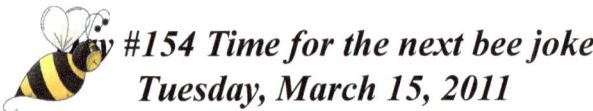 ### #154 Time for the next bee joke
Tuesday, March 15, 2011

Okay. The county I live in is having a special election today for County Commissioner, so try this one:

What's the difference between a beehive and a polling precinct?

Email your answers to me or post them in the comments below (if you can get that to work—grrr!)

BeeAttitude for Day #154: *Blessed are the poll workers, for they are like bees!*

One thing Fran is grateful for right now: *The pot luck lunches we poll workers bring to enjoy*

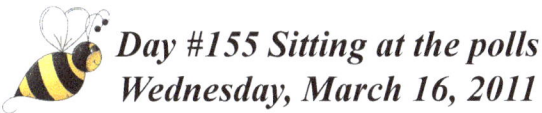 Day #155 Sitting at the polls
Wednesday, March 16, 2011

Yesterday I worked at the polls all day, hoping the roof wouldn't leak (the way it did one year) and hoping we wouldn't have another tornado (like the one we had on election day last November).

For this month's election to replace the somewhat ignominious Chair of the County Commissioners, who chose to resign rather than face an indictment, eight poll workers began work at 6 a.m., when we turned on the machines we'd set up the previous evening, and swore (or affirmed) to uphold our duties as election officials.

By 7:15 we'd had two voters. By noon, there'd still been fewer than a hundred. When the polls closed at 7 p.m., our machines showed that 189 people had voted (out of the 3,533 registered voters in our precinct). Calls to other precinct managers reported similar dismal results. In fact, our precinct was one of the more heavily attended.

Something is wrong with this picture. Five percent of the voters are deciding who will lead Gwinnett County, one of the fastest-growing counties in the nation. Five pathetic percent.

Bees don't do it this way. People who don't know bees, think the queen must lead the hive, but it's really the worker bees—all of them—who make the decisions. The queen doesn't have a vote, and the drones aren't eligible either. Still . . .

100% of the eligible bees
versus
5% of the eligible humans

Humph!

I figure if I don't vote, I don't have the right to complain about the results.

Fran Stewart

Do you vote whenever you have the opportunity?

BeeAttitude for Day #155: *Blessed are those who exercise their civic rights. If they acted like us bees, everyone would behave responsibly.*

One thing Fran is grateful for right now: *Gentle rain.*

Day #156 Two weeks to go till B-Day
Thursday, March 17, 2011

B-Day (Bee Day) in two weeks! or maybe three . . .

And there's still so much to do. We've had so much rain lately that I haven't finished staining the deck yet. Don't want to be slapping stain around while my brand new bees are getting used to their brand new location. So far I have half the deck stained with one coat, and I need two coats over everything.

Then, all those seeds my grandchildren and I started inside are outgrowing their pots, but it's still a bit too early to transplant them outside.

As far as my wonderful work goes, my 6th Biscuit McKee mystery is still in one of its numerous drafts, and I have five amazingly productive doctoral candidates whose dissertations I'm editing, as well as two novels. I'll be leading some classes and doing some book signings and speaking to some book clubs.

On top of all this, Monday night I agreed to serve as the treasurer for the Gwinnett Choral Guild for a two-year term starting in June. Egads! It's a community choir, and I know I really should do my part—which is why I volunteered. But I'm so busy . . .

Can it, Frannie. You're in control of your own calendar. If you're busy, it's your own responsibility, so that's not an acceptable reason to whine.

Okay, okay! But I draw the line HERE. From now on, I'm not volunteering for ANYTHING else.

I'll edit and write. I'll do what's necessary around the house. I'll donate blood every other month. I'll knit and sing. I'll connect with my family and friends. I'll walk and garden and read. I'll uphold my volunteer commitments. I'll play at beekeeping.

Hmm . . . That sounds like a pretty good life, doesn't it?

BeeAttitude for Day #156: *Blessed are they who appreciate their lives, for they shall glow with well-bee-ing.*

What Fran is grateful for right now: *My editing clients*

 ## Day #157 Potatoes in a Garbage Can
Friday, March 18, 2011

I found the coolest book at the library: *Grow Great Grub: organic food from small spaces* by Gayla Trail. It's a good enough book that I plan to buy a copy so I can make notes in the margins. She said I could grow potatoes in a trashcan, as long as it was more than 18" tall. A clean trash can.

So, I unloaded a blue plastic behemoth that's been sitting in this garage for six years and in the one at my previous house for at least ten years. It held odd tools and long scraps of wood, all of which I stashed here and there around the garage, contributing to the overall happy clutter. Drilled some holes in the bottom of the can and filled it with 5" of potting soil.

There were these two already-sprouting potatoes on hand, one of which I found in the back of my refrigerator drawer. *(Don't raise your eyebrows at me. I have a botanically-interesting 'fridge. So there.)*

I cut each potato in several pieces, each with an active eye, and let them dry for a couple of days. Then I plopped them in the can, covered them with another 2 or 3 inches of soil and waited for them to grow up through that layer. I keep piling more dirt on them as they extend upward. Eventually the can will be full, the shoots will leaf out, and finally will flower. That will make my bees happy!

Once the leaves yellow and die back, I'll be able to harvest pounds and pounds of potatoes without having had to do any weeding to speak of. That will make me happy!

The bees win / I win.

Perfect.

Fran Stewart

BeeAttitude for Day #157: *Blessed are people who write helpful books, for they shall be loved by their readers, and we bees shall praise them for the way we benefit.*

One thing Fran is grateful for right now: *My dependable cell phone*

Day #158 The Case of the Disappearing Hosta
Saturday, March 19, 2011

Remember back in the fall (Day #27, November 7, 2010) when my handyman, Mark Hensley of *All Things New* dug out the roots of the azaleas I didn't want (since the flowers can result in toxic honey) and took them home to plant in his yard?

Well, it turned out that he accidentally dug up a hosta that had grown amidst the roots of the azaleas. You know hostas—come late in the autumn, those leaves die back and disappear.

Lo and behold, when Mark came by this quarter, he brought me a big pot with my hosta in it. The shoots surprised him when they started their springtime sprouting.

Mark could have so easily kept the plant, and I never would have known the difference. I would have assumed that it had been destroyed in the azalea-war.

Integrity. The **Mark** of a good person.

BeeAttitude for Day #158: *Blessed are they who prepare a home for us bees, for we shall settle in happily and brighten their days with our buzzing.*

One thing Fran is grateful for right now: *My dependable car*

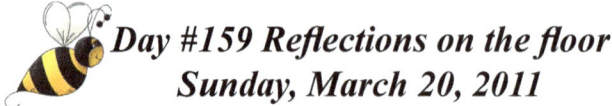
Day #159 Reflections on the floor
Sunday, March 20, 2011

Miss Polly goes nuts every afternoon when the sun shines in through the bay window and hits the plastic sign that hangs from the bottom of a wind chime. Don't worry. I have no plans to enter my house in a decorating competition. At any rate, the sign says:

Writer at Work / Do Not Disturb

Polly pays no attention to the words whatsoever, as she launches herself across the keyboard of my laptop to pounce on the reflection skittering around the room. I must admit that I add to the chaos by blowing a stream of air onto the sign to make it gyrate. *I needed to take a break from that one particular paragraph I was having trouble with anyway, right?*

How do I ever get anything accomplished without hiding in my upstairs office (which happens to be off limits to the cats)?

But the other day I had a disturbing thought. What if the reflections worry the bees? After all, I can clearly see the back deck from this window, and when the sign spins, it reflects light not only onto the inside walls and floor, but also back out the window—crossing over the exact spot where one of the hives is going to sit.

Oh dear! One more thing to worry about! I've heard that bees can get their navigation instincts messed up by cell phone waves. I hope that's not true, because there is absolutely nothing I can do about it. But I *can* position my curtains so they protect the hives from the spurts of reflected light.

Whew! One problem solved.

BeeAttitude for Day #159: *Blessed are those who look at life from our point of view, for they shall become increasingly inventive.*

One thing Fran is grateful for right now: *Fresh organic lettuce from a local farm*

Day #160 You can't beat a good mechanic
Monday, March 21, 2011

Dan Palmer at AutoStop in Buford has been servicing my cars for more than ten years. First it was a little gray Maxima, then it was LadyBug, my red Mitsubishi truck, and now he takes good care of ElliBug, the champagne-colored Nissan—the one who has her very own trophy for "the car with the most polka-dots." (See Day #106 - 1/26/11 for a picture.)

Last week I had an oil change and regular vehicle check, and I got to thinking about how good it is to be able to trust that the person servicing your vehicle will do a good job. That, of course, led me to thinking about bees.

Yes, I know, EVERYTHING leads me to thinking about bees lately.

But bees trust each other to do what needs to be done in the hive. The newly-emerged (and still rather wobbly) baby bee has her specific job, cleaning and polishing the cells, getting them ready for the next round of egg-laying by the queen. It's kind of like the oil-change of the bee world.

As she gets a bit older and her exoskeleton hardens a bit, she begins to care for the brood (those are the newly-hatched and very hungry larvae), feeding them royal jelly for 3 days. For the next 3 days, she feeds them regular old worker food, sometimes called *bee milk*. But this little bee is not simply pulling bee milk from a faucet. Nope. She has to manufacture it from glands in her head.

During those 6 days, each larva increases **500** times in size. That takes a lot of bee milk from those dedicated little workers.

The worker bee still has lots more jobs to go through during her lifespan. But those will wait until tomorrow's blog.

BeeAttitude for Day #160: *Blessed are those who know how to repair things, for they shall be ever safe.*

One thing Fran is grateful for right now: *The fresh lettuce I ate from my own garden!*

[***2019 Note****: Autostop is yet another small business that, like the bookstore I mentioned recently, bit the dust.]*

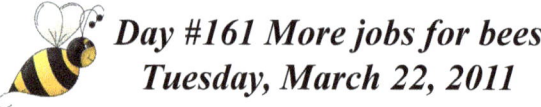
Day #161 More jobs for bees
Tuesday, March 22, 2011

We left off yesterday with the little nurse bees feeding the larvae for six days. At that point, slightly older bees move in to cap off the larval cell so the pupae (that's what they're called at this point) can continue growing for 12 days into a baby bee. Those babies emerge and start cleaning cells.

Meanwhile, the nurse bees have gone on to other jobs. Up until they're about 20 days old, they'll be capping cells, constructing new comb, tending the queen, guarding the entrance to the hive, fanning the hive to heat or cool it as necessary, accepting nectar and pollen brought in by the forager bees, and packing it into cells, and curing the nectar into honey.

During their busy days, they also have to find the time to take orientation flights, circling the hive until they can recognize it from any angle. Gradually their flights get longer, so they can always find their way back home.

All this in three short weeks.

After that, the glands that produce wax and larval food have shriveled up, so the bees become foragers, traveling up to five miles from the hive to find nectar and pollen.

And it takes twelve bees to make one teaspoon of honey. If you're ever lucky enough to get some **Bees Knees Honey**, you'd better appreciate all the work that went into it!

BeeAttitude for Day #161: *Blessed are those who do their jobs well, for their hive shall thrive.*

One thing Fran is grateful for right now: *The pole bean plants that are beginning to twine up and up.*

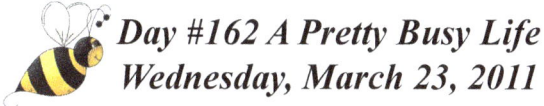 Day #162 A Pretty Busy Life
Wednesday, March 23, 2011

I heard from H & L Bee Farm, saying that the pick-up date for the bees probably won't be until April 10th. Part of me says *phooey* because I want to get them sooner, but another part of me is relieved. There's still so much to do before they get here.

With all this rain I haven't finished staining the deck yet.

It's still a bit too early to transplant the various veggies and flowers my grandchildren and I started indoors.

My still-unused branding iron from Brand New is waiting patiently in what used to be the family room but is steadily being transferred into the Bee Equipment Launching Pad.

On top of work (5 doctoral dissertations and 2 novels to edit, plus my own book to write, a seminar presentation to prepare, and some book clubs to speak to), there's the volunteer position I agreed to as the treasurer for the choral guild. Everybody's busy, so the simple fact that I'm busy is not an excuse, as I've mentioned before.

How do bees ever manage to go through all their chores? Oh, uh, yeah. They do only one job at a time, and then they move on to the next job. You can refer back to the previous two days to see what those jobs are.

BeeAttitude for Day #162: *Blessed are those who know what they want to do in life, for they shall be infinitely satisfied.*

One thing Fran is grateful for right now: *My comfy old sweatpants*

Day #163 Puns at the Soccer Game
Thursday, March 24, 2011

I can't think of anything stupendous to write about, so I'm going to tell you about what happened last Saturday on the sidelines of my grandson's soccer game.

My co-grandparents and I stood there cheering until Bill Martin, known to all the grandkids as Paw-Paw, said he had to ask me a question. "Sure," I said. He glanced apologetically at his wife and asked, "Do bees poop?"

Now, this was a logical question coming from someone who is a family doctor (intestinal information fascinates docs) and also from someone who doesn't read my blog. He came from the hospital to the soccer game. He's always caring for a patient. He founded (and is the head doc at) the Hope Clinic in Lawrenceville. How could he possibly find time to read blog posts?

So, he didn't know about my blog entry #86 (January 6, 2011) where I explain about cleansing flights. If you missed that one, you might want to look it up.

At any rate, we stood there making bee-poop jokes and missed the last three goals of the game. As the final whistle blew, I said, "Whoops! We haven't been watching!"—at which point Bill said, "Guess you'll give us all a stinging reprimand."

It went on from there, but I'll save the rest of the puns for another time—when I can remember what they were. The good thing about not recalling punch lines is that every joke I hear seems brand new to me, since I can't remember what's coming.

BeeAttitude for Day #163: *Blessed are the grandparents, for they shall have grand-fun in life.*

One thing Fran is grateful for right now: *The morning glory I planted next to Faye, who grows near the corner of my deck. Yes, of course I name my trees and flowering vines.*

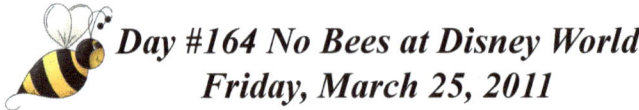 Day #164 No Bees at Disney World
Friday, March 25, 2011

I've just returned from four days in Florida. Yes, even though it was a vacation, I took my laptop so I could post each day. And no, I didn't mention Disney because I feel funny telling the world that my house is unattended (except for a wonderful friend who stops by frequently to take care of my cats any time I'm out of state).

There's a lovely flower show going on in Epcot Center. And I spent most of the time looking for honeybees. I didn't see a single one. I guess they can't encourage bees there because of the thousands of people who might bother the bees by flailing their arms around. Still, with all the busy-ness going on around me, the place seemed oddly silent without any little buzz-ers flying around. Disney doesn't seem to welcome bees.

The good news: there were bees in the 3-D program *It's Tough to be a Bug* at Animal Kingdom.

You've probably been there—maybe many times—so I don't need to talk about all the goings-on in WDW. My feet may take a few days to recover; you know that feeling.

Did I have a good time? Yes.

Am I happy to be home? Yes.

Will my bees have a happy welcome here when they arrive? **YES!**

BeeAttitude for Day #164: *Blessed are those who welcome bees to their flowers, for they shall have the music of our buzzing.*

One thing Fran is grateful for right now: *The Animal Kingdom employee whose eyes lit up when she told us about her favorite white rhinos.*

BeesKnees #2: A Beekeeping Memoir

 ### *Day #165 A Gentle Approach to Beekeeping*
Saturday, March 26, 2011

I found yet another good beekeeping book and have been entranced with the philosophical attitude of the author. Ross Conrad wrote *Natural Beekeeping: organic approaches to modern apiculture* to put together in one book all the information it took him years to accumulate as he was mentored by various beekeepers.

That's one great thing about beekeepers. There's no such thing as too many bees, and every beekeeper I've spoken to has been delighted to share information with me.

Here's a gem I found in the first chapter:

"The honeybee inspires me to work into my daily life this lesson: that we should take what we need to live in the world in such a way that we give something back and improve upon things, thus making the world a better place."
—Ross Conrad

He said that when he went into the bee yard with no protective clothing on, he had to adjust his attitude to one of ease and grace so as not to alarm the bees. When he did that—when he was careful not to hurt them or frighten them—they responded gently to his presence. But when he went in there suited up as if he were afraid of an attack, he was less careful, ended up hurting bees through his inattention, and consequently was stung as the bees reacted to his carelessness.

That made me glad about my bee-clothing choices. I do think I'll be more comfortable with a veil on at first. But with my long-sleeved white shirt and long white pants (the ones I bought at Good Will several months ago), I think I'll be just fine. I haven't bought any gloves, because when I had a chance to remove that frame from Rob Alexander's hive a couple of weeks ago, I needed all the dexterity available—and that would not have been possible with gloves. I would have been accidentally squashing bees right and left, releasing those death pheromones that indicate a threat to the hive. No wonder some beekeepers get stung a lot.

BeeAttitude for Day #165: *Blessed are those who approach the hive as if they were on our side, for we shall respond to them gently.*

One thing Fran is grateful for right now: *The half-barrel I'm going to grow my morning glories in.*

And Cowan's Book Nook in East Ellijay, GA, where I'll be signing my books today. Stop by and say hello—and buy some books (no matter who wrote them!)

Day #166 Hive Autopsies
Sunday, March 27, 2011

I've been reading about how to do a hive autopsy—that's the process for figuring out why all the bees in a hive died off.

I hope I never have to use this knowledge. *Natural Beekeeping*, the book I bought recently, has a chart (I love well-organized charts) with all the symptoms in the left column and the probable causes in the right. The last symptom on the list, caused by **pesticides or chemical poisonings** is: "Sudden collapse of the hive. Numerous dead bees lying around in front of the hive with their tongues sticking out" (p. 61).

If that image isn't enough to stop you from using pesticides on your lawns and gardens, I don't know what will. The thought of all my brave little worker bees dying, gasping for air, with their little tongues flailing, brings tears to my eyes – and I don't even have my bees yet.

BeeAttitude for Day #166: *Blessed are those who refuse to buy pesticides, for they shall contribute to the health of Mother Earth, and the world will be a better place for them and for us, the bees.*

One thing Fran is grateful for right now: *Cowan's Book Nook in Ellijay, where I signed my books yesterday. They're having to close that store (not enough sales), but they will keep their store in Blue Ridge GA open.*
FRANattitude for Day #166
 Blessed are those who buy books from real bookstores, for they shall help keep that breed alive and well.

[**2019 Note:** The store in Ellijay eventually closed as well. Sometimes I feel like this whole 600-day blog post idea has been a breeding ground for announcing the failure of small businesses. On the other hand, there are still a lot of thriving local stores that I make a point of supporting. I hope you do the same.]

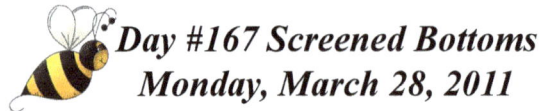
Day #167 Screened Bottoms
Monday, March 28, 2011

Check one more thing off my to-do list! Sunday I managed to staple screening onto the bottom of the hive body that will play home to my package of bees in a couple of weeks. I haven't been able to find any screening with 1/8" squares, so I took two layers of ¼" screening and offset them, then stapled them in place. I hope it works the way it's supposed to.

The idea is that the various little mites and beetles that bother bees will fall out of the hive through the screening on the bottom. I can just see me going on beetle-patrol, stepping on those suckers when I find them underneath the hives. The screening is supposed to be fine enough, however, to keep out robber bees from other hives. It will also prevent mice from crawling up through the bottom.

Sunday was a busy day. I dug up some hostas to give to my daughter and to my friend Millie, then planted buckwheat in their place. Presumably, buckwheat flowers last longer than hosta blooms, so the bees ought to be happier. It seems as if everything I do lately ends with the thought *I hope this works*.

BeeAttitude for Day #167: *Blessed are those who try, for they shall succeed sometimes.*

One thing Fran is grateful for right now: *The New American Shakespeare Tavern, where I saw* Two Noble Kinsman *last night. One more play to go (*Edward III *next week), and I will have seen all 39 plays by (or attributed to) Shakespeare.*

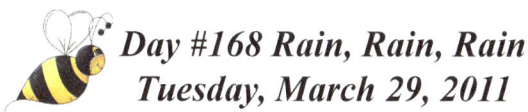 Day #168 Rain, Rain, Rain
Tuesday, March 29, 2011

Other than a short break on Sunday, just long enough for me to dig up those hostas, it's been raining since last Saturday, and I just read that it's supposed to keep going, with thunderstorms no less, at least through Thursday.

Other than the inconvenience of trying to keep the bird feeders filled without getting the seed soaked, rainy days have never bothered me. All in all, I enjoy cloudy days and rainy days. Maybe it's because I have *vitiligo*, a condition where there is little or no melanin in the skin, so there's nothing to protect me from the burning rays of the sun. I go through most of the year with long sleeves or a sunbrella. Yes, that's a word. I invented it.

The floods in 2009 weren't any fun, but my neighborhood was safe, even when the creek that runs through my back yard grew from a gentle two feet wide to a raging torrent that I measured (after the floods were over) at more than 50 feet wide. It was easy to measure. The plants were all bent sideways.

But now, with my bees arriving in a couple of weeks, I'm beginning to see rain in a different way. If my bees were here, now, in all this rain, at the end of winter with their honey stores somewhat depleted before the strong nectar and pollen flows begin, they'd be pretty unhappy, fairly restless, and possibly awfully hungry.

Think about it. If you can't fly in the rain because the water weighs down your wings, and you're stuck in one room with 20 or 30 thousand sisters, wouldn't you get a bit grumpy?

BeeAttitude for Day #168: *Blessed are those who are patient, for they shall eventually get what they need.*

Fran Stewart

One thing Fran is grateful for right now: *The squirrel-guards on the birdfeeder poles. So far, they've kept the squirrels on the ground, cleaning up the fallen seed.*

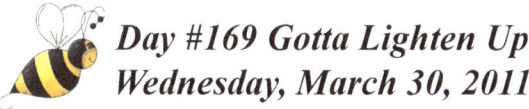 *Day #169 Gotta Lighten Up*
Wednesday, March 30, 2011

Okay. I'm tired of grumping about the rain and worrying about what it's doing to bees throughout the area. And the birds shaking off their wet feathers and trying to find food. And the various animals, and people, too, who are caught unavoidably in the rain.

So, here are some pictures I took last week to remind us all that weather does change if we wait long enough.

Delphiniums at Epcot Center

and

a friend I met underground at Animal Kingdom

And I need to remember that one of the hummingbirds in my yard perched on top of a birdfeeder pole and took a glorious bath in the deluge—shaking her feathers and wobbling her head around and obviously enjoying her shower immensely.

BeeAttitude for Day #169: *Blessed are the patient, for they shall eventually be recompensed.*

One thing Fran is grateful for right now: *a dependable camera*

BeesKnees #2: A Beekeeping Memoir

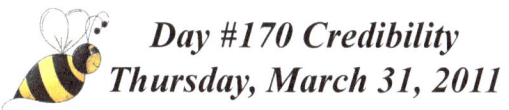
Day #170 Credibility
Thursday, March 31, 2011

In 1938, Bodog F. Beck, M.D. and Doreé Smedley wrote *Honey & Your Health*. The subtitle was *a nutrimental, medicinal and historical commentary.*

Sounds great, eh?

They start out talking about the ways honey has been used in the thousands of years that people have known about honey.

- A pot of honey on the breakfast table is one of the oldest traditions that is still in effect for many people.
- Egyptian tombs show paintings of folks harvesting honey using smoke as an aid
- Ancient Greeks thought regular eating of honey would help them to live longer
- Ancient Romans held honey-harvest feasts, much like our modern-day Thanksgiving
- Honey was often used as a medium of exchange, all the more reason to celebrate the harvest, because honey meant prosperity.

So far, all of this sounds credible. I haven't gotten to the part yet about how honey is used successfully in the treatment of all sorts of medical conditions, although I've browsed through the book and found many statements I concur with.

But then, I glanced at page 80. "The average back-lot beekeeper of a small city or town harvests between fifty and one hundred pounds of surplus honey a season."

That sounded about right. Beck and Smedley lost points with me, though, when they wrote that, in an area with abundant nectar plants, an industrious beekeeper, who was willing to learn the most up-to-date methods, could "increase this yield to two hundred pounds of honey a season **per hive.**" Maybe I'm overly pessimistic, but that sounds way too high to me.

They went on to say that under "special conditions and ideal management, the yield may be stepped up to three hundred or even five hundred pounds per hive." Grrr! Do you know how hard a beekeeper would have to push a hive to get that much honey? **Over-management is one of the factors in the Colony Collapse Disorder that's been rampant in this country.** European countries have not experienced CCD. Doesn't that tell you something right there?

Greedy people trying to get every possible dollar out of their hives ought to be strung up by their toes. A **truly** good management practice (respecting the natural way bees operate) gives the bees a break and results in a reasonable amount of honey per hive.

So, Beck and Smedley, I'll read your recipes for good health and maybe follow a good many of them, but I'm going to ignore that other bunk you wrote.

BeeAttitude for Day #170: *Blessed are they who give us a break and let us behave naturally, for their honey shall be infused with love and good health.*

One thing Fran is grateful for right now: *Honey on toast*

Day #171 Public Edict
Please Read for Your Own Edification
Friday, Apr. 1, 2011

In the interest of the public good, the following edict is hereby issued:

WHEREAS: beekeeping has been established as an activity of great monetary benefit to this community, considering the increased harvests of fruits, flowers, and vegetables that result from pollination by the honeybee (*Apis mellifera*), and

WHEREAS: beekeepers have been shown to be a bastion of rectitude in their fight to protect the species of *Apis mellifera* from the depredations of chemicals, predators, and weather, and

WHEREAS: said honeybees have had an uphill battle lately where said weather, predators, and chemicals are concerned,

THEREFORE, be it hereby known that from this date and heretofore, all persons not associated with an established hive of bees will, within the next thirty (30) days, be subject to imprisonment of not more than eighty (80) days, and a fine of $24,197.36, this amount being the estimated yearly value of a honeybee hive to the community.

If, THEREFORE, a citizen does not keep at least one hive of bees, said citizen will be expected to reimburse the community for the dollars lost to that community and to suffer such retribution as shall be deemed necessary, to wit—imprisonment for eighty (80) days. During said imprisonment, said prisoner shall be fed only those foods which have not resulted, either directly or indirectly, from the pollination activities of *Apis mellifera*, to wit: water. Chewing on wisps of hay will be allowed, since grasses are pollinated by the wind.

THIS DECREE issued in accordance with the laws of this state and this county and this nation on the <u>first</u> of <u>April</u> in the year <u>2011</u>, and hereby attested to by narF trawetS, Clerk of the Court.

BeeAttitude for Day #171: *Blessed are those who appreciate the value of us bees, for we shall refrain from stinging them.*

Fran Stewart

One thing Fran is grateful for right now: *My good friend, narF trawetS, born on this first of April. Happy Birthday, narF!*

Day #172 SciFri
Saturday, Apr. 2, 2011

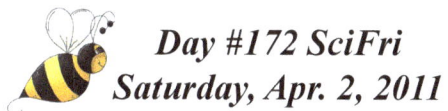

Cathy Akers-Jordan, a regular reader of **BeeKnees** sent me a link to a website called ScienceFriday.com. They produce weekly snippets of very interesting science. This particular link was about bees and a type of orchid that takes advantage of the bees by bombing them with pollen. Thanks, Cathy! I loved those slow-motion photos of the plant at work.

Pollen Grain (magnified)

But then I saw another SciFri post listed on the left. *Pollen Origami* was the name. Well, of course I had to open it and watch the video. [2019 Note: That original video no longer exists—or at least not where I can find it. But here's underlined another link that will give you an idea of how the folding happens.] The Atlanta area gets a lot of pollen in the spring – a fact that I'm sure my bees will appreciate. I figure I ought to know as much about pollen as I could. Plus, I just love learning new things.

The idea is that the inside of a pollen grain dries out very easily, so the impermeable outside layer folds itself around the inside in an origami-like process, forming a waterproof protection. Fascinating!

BeeAttitude for Day #172: *Blessed are the people who plant lots of pollen-bearing flowers and trees for us, for they shall live in the middle of glory.*

One thing Fran is grateful for right now: *Whoever invented Weetabix. I know it's more expensive than Shredded Wheat, but I don't care. I like it. [Now you know what I ate for breakfast yesterday!]*

Fran Stewart

Day #173 Whew!
The yellow world around Atlanta
Sunday, Apr. 3, 2011

Busy day Saturday. I got the cinder blocks set up on the deck so I can put the hives on them. The hives need to be off the ground so any varroa mites and small hive beetles will fall through the screened bottom onto the wood below (where I can squash them).

I spent a fair amount of time making sure there was enough room around the blocks so I could get my broom in there to sweep off the porcupine eggs. For those of you who don't live under a sweet-gum tree, those spiny seedpods drop by the thousands—yes, thousands—year-round, making a barefoot romp through the yard an impossibility.

And of course, this is the time of year when the whole Atlanta area is bombarded with pine pollen. Not just a little bit. A LOT! When I moved here almost 20 years ago, I thought the street was running with urine after the first spring rain, but it was just all that bright yellow pollen swirling along the streets.

The yellow polka dot spots on my car don't show up as much now. The good news is that my hives won't look pollen-covered at all, since they're yellow to begin with.

The plants I put in a few days ago are doing well. And some bees from the neighborhood stopped by to take a sip. The way I chose the plants at the garden center was simple: I looked for the plants that had bees working on them!

And, the best news of all—my bluebird house has babies in it!

BeeAttitude for Day #173: *Blessed are the plants that make pollen for us to collect, for we shall spread their bounty.*

One thing Fran is grateful for right now: *My garage*

FRANattitude for the day: I have used entirely too many exclamation points in this post. My inner editor cringes when I do that. On the other hand, I'm happy! and I'm excited about the bees! and the plants! and the baby birds (!!!)

 ### Day #174 Honey Medicine
Monday, Apr. 4, 2011

I've been reading a book called *Honey: Gourmet Medicine* by Joe Traynor. I bought it through Mann Lake, a beekeeping supply company.

Very interesting information about the ways in which honey can be used to combat diseases and disorders. That sort of information isn't valued much in this country, since we seem to be at the mercy of the pharmaceutical industry.

Don't get me wrong. There is a place for antibiotics. But using them as a first line of defense instead of as a last resort has led to the creation of super-microbes, resistant to almost any medicine we can throw at them.

Honey, on the other hand, does not attack germs, so it doesn't lead to any sort of resistance. It simply creates an environment where the germs cannot live. Smart, eh? Traynor even referred to a doctor in the 30s who used honey to treat patients who had cataracts. A drop of honey in each eye at night (even though it stings a bit), and rinse the eye out in the morning. Cataracts gone. It sounded like a good idea to me, and if it worked, would sure beat surgery.

The trouble with honey is that anyone can access it, and it can't be patented, so it's not worth the efforts of the drug industry to package.

I use it on scratches and cuts to prevent infection.

Give it a try. It's medicine you can eat.

BeeAttitude for Day #174: *Blessed are those who give honey a try, for they shall live in better health.*

One thing Fran is grateful for right now: *My e-book royalties. I'm so glad people are reading my books!*

Fran Stewart

Day #175 Trail Dames and a Bee at Stone Mountain
Tuesday, Apr. 5, 2011

Now that I have pictures to include, I can tell you about the hike I went on, around the base of Stone Mountain, with the Trail Dames.

I found out about Trail Dames last year, when Susan Larson, a columnist with the Gwinnett Daily Post, wrote about the founder of the group.

What can I say . . . it's for women who—like yours truly—are out of shape. I went on one hike last fall and thoroughly enjoyed the challenge. The trail was one fairly easy mile to a gorgeous waterfall, then about a quarter-mile straight up. Well, maybe not *straight* up, but I did have to crawl part of the way and clamber over fallen trees. Half the group had stayed behind to swim at the waterfall (brrr!) and the rest of us tackled the trek to the upper falls.

I slept very well that night.

Two days ago, at 8 a.m., I met up with the group again for a trek around Stone Mountain.

Twenty-two people, most of them decked out in real hiking boots and toting real backpacks, some with hoses attached to inner water reservoirs so they could sip as they went along. Two dogs—Molly, shown here, and Buster, who led the trek.

Then there was Frannie. I wore a comfortable old pair of tennis shoes, carried a walking stick with a carved turtle at the top (I'd bought it at Gwinnett Environmental & Heritage Center last year), and lugged along my granddaughter's old book-bag from fourth grade. I figured if I got left behind, they could spot the bright turquoise bag strapped to my back. Here I am (in the green shirt) at the rear end as some of us posed on one of the bridges.

You see, I'd volunteered for the "sweep" position—bringing up the rear to be sure nobody got left behind. I was concerned, though, that I'd lag so far behind, they'd forget about me. Not to worry. There were a few others as slow as I, and we dawdled along quite happily, enjoying the imposing bulk of Stone Mountain (seen here behind a tracery of bare tree branches), the gorgeous azaleas, and a bunch of wildflowers.

Fran Stewart

Did I mention the trek was **five and a half miles**? That's a long way, for somebody who hasn't walked that far in, oh, about 40 years. Who am I kidding? I've *never* walked that far before. But, I did it, and saw some wonderful sights along the way, as you can see from all these pictures that Cheryl Bharath and Laura James took. I copied them (with permission) from the Trail Dames website. If you look at this picture very carefully, you can see a bee in there. Yes. You can. Definitely.

Check out the Trail Dames and come join us on an upcoming hike. I survived this one. The next one will be a breeze.

BeeAttitude for Day #175: *Blessed are those who prepare a lovely home for us, for we shall be content and make lots of honey.*

One thing Fran is grateful for right now: *Joan, who carried my pack for me the last quarter mile.*

Day #176 Stained!
Wednesday, Apr. 6, 2011

Finally! Finally, the weather cooperated enough for me to finish staining the uprights on the deck. Now I won't have to worry about the bees getting their little feet stuck in yucky stain.

And while I was rummaging around in the garage, I came across an outdoor re-circulating fountain that a neighbor gave me six years ago when I moved into this house. It needed some work, and I hadn't had time to fiddle with it, so I'd stuck it aside and eventually buried it under other junk. Why do I collect so much stuff in my garage? Do you do that, too? Still, I repaired it and set it up on the deck, so now there's a fountain that drips a drop every second or so. The birds will enjoy it, I think.

I still need to buy one more cinder block so I can set the hives up off the deck surface, and then I'll be ready. We're almost there: Bee-Day is on the horizon!

BeeAttitude for Day #176: *Blessed are those who are hungry for knowledge, for they shall find enjoyment all around them.*

What Fran is grateful for right now: *Bluebirds, cardinals, downy woodpeckers, pine siskins, Eastern towhees, chickadees, goldfinches, hummingbirds, and tufted titmice, plus all the others I don't know the names of.*

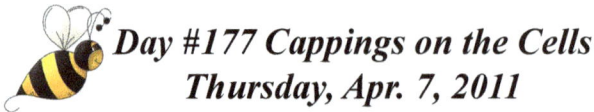

Day #177 Cappings on the Cells
Thursday, Apr. 7, 2011

I can't wait to see the different types of cell capping that will be in the hive once my bees get busy.

Cells that are capped (covered over) with **brownish wax** hold the brood, the baby bees.

White caps indicate honey within. And I still feel somewhat nervous about how I'm ever going to deal with extracting the honey from the frames. But I'll deal with that when the time comes.

Big fat dome-like cappings mean that there are baby drones within.

Cells packed with **yellow stuff** but not capped over hold the pollen, which provides protein for the babies.

I'll be getting them next week. Can I borrow a camera from somebody, and will you come take the pictures while I'm trying to convince 12,000 bees to go into a yellow box?

BeeAttitude for Day #177: *Blessed are the environmentally-minded, for they shall help make this world a better place for all of us bees – and for you people, too.*

One thing Fran is grateful for right now: *Being able to figure out PowerPoint for a writer's seminar/webinar I'll be teaching on April 16th*

Day #178 Feeling Encouraged
Friday, Apr. 8, 2011

We had a Board meeting last night, where we sat over dinner and discussed what we want the Gwinnett Beekeepers Club to accomplish over the next year. It was lovely to see the enthusiasm of the other members. Each of us wants to encourage beekeeping and to educate people about the value of honeybees.

But the real value for me came when I mentioned that I'll be picking up my bees next week. Instantly the experienced beekeepers were full of suggestions
- stay calm,
- be sure you take pictures because this is the only time you'll open a package of bees for the FIRST time,
- make sure the queen cage is placed in the middle of the hive body,
- spray the bees a little bit—not too much, and
- enjoy the process.

That was the big one—enjoy the process. It won't help the bees one bit if I get all nervous and flustered. So, I have my checklist all made out, and I honestly think I'm as ready as I possibly can be.

Tomorrow I'm going to call the bee supply place to see if I can get an exact date for picking up my bees. Then I'll be twiddling my thumbs, waiting for the big day and wondering if there's anything I've forgotten. Maybe I'm *not* as ready as I think I am ...

BeeAttitude for Day #178: *Blessed are those who stay calm, for they shall not upset us.*

One thing Fran is grateful for right now: *Doggie bags from restaurants.*

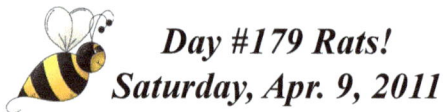

Day #179 Rats!
Saturday, Apr. 9, 2011

Friday morning I called H & L Bee Farm to be sure I could pick up my bees next week, and they said that half their shop had been destroyed by a tornado. Fortunately, nobody was hurt and only a few hives were blown over, but they're still in a tizzy trying to get organized to put the packages of bees together.
GROAN
It may be another couple of weeks before I can pick up my girls.
ANOTHER GROAN

Still, let's look on the bright side.
-This way my bees will be avoiding all the heavy winds and thunderstorms that have beset Gwinnett County over the last week and look to be continuing for another few days at least.
-My garden plants will be that much taller and that much closer to needing pollination.
-The Mack truck that would have run me down if I'd driven to Ocilla this week will be somewhere else altogether when I drive down there later this month—see, the tornado at H&L saved my life!
-I'll have the time to watch that *Installing Your Package of Bees* DVD a couple more times, so I'll be that much more ready.

Okay, now I feel better.

BeeAttitude for Day #179: *Blessed are those who see the bright side, for they shall avoid discouragement. If we bees got discouraged, nothing would ever be sweet!*

One thing Fran is grateful for right now: *Fudge made with honey. Yum!*

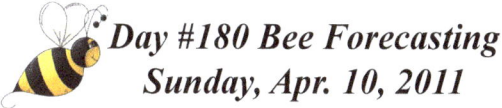 Day #180 Bee Forecasting
Sunday, Apr. 10, 2011

I visited someone (who prefers to remain anonymous) a while back, and when we walked up near her beehives, she said, "The girls are pretty happy today."

How could she tell, I asked, as skeptical as this cow.

"Well, they just sound happy, don't you think?"

It reminded me of my brother-in-law, a retired wheat farmer. Ask him what the weather will be like for the next few days, and instead of looking at the newspaper or the TV, he'll wander outside, look up, take a sniff or two, and deliver his prediction, which most times turns out to be exactly right.

Someday I hope I know my bees as well as Marvin knows the breeze.

BeeAttitude for Day #180: *Blessed are the weather forecasters, for they shall provide endless entertainment.*

One thing Fran is grateful for right now: *My umbrella*

Day #181 Grandma's Irises
Monday, Apr. 11, 2011

My father's mother was a Mississippi farm wife. One of the most poignant memories of my childhood is my watching her on her knees, wearing an old blue faded sunbonnet, weeding her iris garden. I wanted so much to help her, but she was not the sort of grandmother to encourage anyone to poach on her precious time alone with her flowers.

Grandma Stewart's Irises

Long after Grandma's death, I visited my Aunt Mary, who had taken some of the irises from her mother's garden and planted them at her own place in Tennessee, where they had multiplied into enormous beds of deep purple, light lavender, and multi-colored wonder. Aunt Mary gave some of each color to me, and I planted them at my house in Suwanee. Then, when I moved to my current house here on the other side of Hog Mountain, I lugged irises along with me, leaving plenty for the enjoyment of the people who'd bought my house.

Fran Stewart

Yesterday I was out in the front yard, filling the bird feeder, and I saw that several of Grandma's irises had shot up those distinctive tall stems, topped with furled buds. This is what some of them looked like the spring after I moved into this house. Now these particular ones have pink dianthus growing around their feet.

I hope my bees will enjoy them as much as I do when they finally bloom again this year.

One thing Fran is grateful for right now: *My grandchildren, who are always welcome to share my joys.*

Day #182 Oh Dear! Too Many Flower Choices?
Tuesday, Apr. 12, 2011

I just read that honeybees have a tendency to focus on one particular type of flower at a time, which is why it's possible to have clover honey/ macadamia nut honey / sourgum honey / tupelo honey and such like. And here I am planting all sorts of different flowers and veggies in my yard so my bees will have lots of choices.

It seems like every time I read something lately, it makes hash of what I read last week or last month. Isn't it great to know there are so many people experimenting with different ways of keeping the bees happy?

So, I'm going to keep on planting the flowers and shrubs that I love, and the bees will figure out how to deal with it.

BeeAttitude for Day #182: *Blessed are those who love us enough to plant delicious flowers for us, for we shall enjoy whatever they plant and shall pollinate it well.*

One thing Fran is grateful for right now: *The Gwinnett Choral Guild. I love singing with them.*

[**2019 Note**: It's not that bees focus on one type of flower at a time. Instead, they gather from whatever is the most abundant source of nectar at any given time. If the bees are in the middle of an orange grove, they'll produce orange-flower honey. If they're close to a lot of sourgum trees that are in bloom, they'll produce the rich dark sourgum honey. Any honey produced when all sorts of flowers are abundant will result in what's called wildflower honey.]

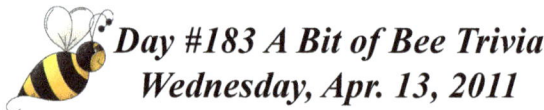
Day #183 A Bit of Bee Trivia
Wednesday, Apr. 13, 2011

Why is a honeybee not a honey bee?

A few examples to illustrate the difference:

- A dragonfly is not a type of fly, so it is not a dragon fly
- Ladybugs are not bugs; they are beetles. So they are not lady bugs.

A honeybee is a bee that produces honey, so the correct term (regardless of what terms I've used in this blog so far) is two-worded: honey bee.

Despite all this, I still prefer the single word *honeybee*. So that's what I'll keep on using.

BeeAttitude for Day #183: *Blessed are the wordsmiths, for they shall call us wondrous things.*

One thing Fran is grateful for right now: *My dear friend Debby Barker, who has the most amazing healing energy.*

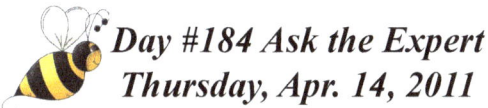 Day #184 Ask the Expert
Thursday, Apr. 14, 2011

They're right – a little knowledge IS a dangerous thing.

Tuesday evening, the Gwinnett Beekeepers Club hosted Dr. James Ellis, from the University of Florida. He brought his boundless enthusiasm for entomology, and a Power Point show so we could visualize what he was talking about.

All those things I've been telling you about small cell foundation – absolutely no scientific basis to it at all. Jim said that most of the beliefs about honeybees are based on hearsay. "This is what I hear, so I'll say it again" . . . and suddenly it's believed to be scientific fact. His department tests all sorts of things about honeybees, so he ought to know.

Still, I cling to the belief that small cell foundation is the way to go – simply because it's closer to the way the honeybees would build their comb if people weren't interfering. So, I'll use the SCF, whether or not it encourages the bees to be more happy and healthy than they would be on the super-duper size.

At least Dr. Jim said I wouldn't hurt the bees one way or the other. Good!

I didn't happen to mention to him about hearing that singing to the bees keeps them calmer. If I'd told him that, he probably would have rolled his eyes. I'll just do my singing anyway, but I'm not going to tell anyone – except you – that I'm doing it.

BeeAttitude for Day #184: *Blessed are those who sing to us regardless of what the experts say, for happy singers are always blessed.*

One thing Fran is grateful for right now: *The Atlanta Pen Women, who met in our nature garden at Stone Mountain yesterday and wrote lots of haiku. We also laughed a lot.*

 Day #185 Never Bounce a Bee
Friday, Apr. 15, 2011

"*Whaddya mean* Never Bounce a Bee?"

"*Just what I said, never Bounce a bee.*"

"*Why not?*"

"*I thought you'd never ask...*"

One of the major benefits of bees to humans is their ability to pollinate plants. I always thought they just brushed against the pollen and some of it stuck to them. But last Tuesday at the Gwinnett Beekeepers Club meeting, I found out from Dr. Jim Ellis that the hair on a bee's body is electrostatically charged – like all those balloons we rubbed against our heads when we were kids so we could stick them to the wall.

So, you'd never want to put a sheet of Bounce® in a bee hive, because taking away the static would make it impossible for the bees to collect all those tons of pollen.

Ain't science grand?

p.s. Wait till you see what myth I'll be exploding in tomorrow's blog. Jim Ellis was a goldmine of information.

BeeAttitude for Day #185: *Blessed are the good scientists, for they explain things to our humans so they can treat us better.*

One thing Fran is grateful for right now: *Perseverance, the quality that allowed me to figure out how to put together a PowerPoint presentation for the writer's seminar I'll be teaching Saturday.*

 Day #186 How Many Queens in a Hive?
Saturday, Apr. 16, 2011

Dr. Jim Ellis asked us that question, and we all got it wrong. Another myth exploded.

Everything I've ever read has told me that a queen bee will kill all her rivals (any other queens). But Jim asked us this:

Why does a beekeeper think there's only one queen in a hive?

Answer: Because the beekeeper stops counting when s/he finds the first queen.

Well, doggone it. That's right. Every time I've seen beekeepers looking for their queen, they find her and say, "There she is – now let's close up this hive so we don't disturb her too much."

Jim's researchers at the Honeybee Lab at the University of Florida don't stop looking when they find the first queen. Sometimes, they say, there are two or even three queens in a hive.

Amazing, isn't it?

BeeAttitude for Day #186: *Blessed are the queen bees, for they are our mothers.*

Forty-two-thousand things Fran is grateful for right now: *The bees I'll be picking up TOMORROW!*

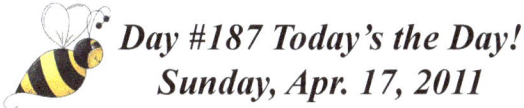 Day #187 Today's the Day! Sunday, Apr. 17, 2011

It's gonna happen, finally, after all this **waiting** and **hoping** and **studying** and **dreaming** and **planning** and **building** and **staining** and **setting up**.

Once my 42,000 new friends are installed in their new home, I'll let you know how it went. Please send encouraging thoughts to all the bees who've spent the night cooped up in a box, waiting for me to arrive, to transport them, and eventually to release them.

BeeAttitude for Day #187: *Blessed are you, and blessed is this day, and all is well in this hive.*

One thing Fran is grateful for right now: *EllieBug (my car), who has never before carried 42,001 passengers. She's pretty strong, isn't she?*

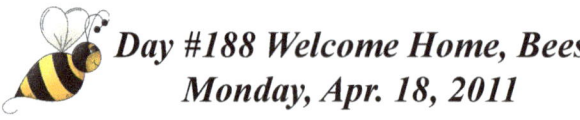
Day #188 Welcome Home, Bees
Monday, Apr. 18, 2011

Just think about it.
After all the books I've read,
- all the beekeepers I've listened to,
- all the DVDs I've watched,
- all the seminars I've taken, and
- all the lists I've made,
you'd think that I'd remember to follow the procedure step-by step.

Sunday morning I got up before 5:00, ate breakfast, and drove 3½ hours to Ocilla GA. I got lost only once, but not for too long, at that.

I'd taken a hive net with me – remember, I blogged about it way back when I first bought it. The idea was to put it in my car, set the nuc and the package on it, draw the string tight at the top, and then drive home with blatant unconcern, knowing that any loose bees would be confined.

Did I use it? No. The lid of the nuc was screwed on tight – no way for the bees to get out of there. So I set the small nucleus hive on the blanket I'd put on my front seat, and blithely told the bee guy to set the package on the floor. He did.

BeesKnees #2: A Beekeeping Memoir

photo credit: Kara Dunn

I got in the car and took off down the road. Once I was back on I-75 North, I heard something buzz beside my ear. It hadn't occurred to me that a great number of bees had been clinging to the **outside** of the package. I'd thought they were all on the **inside**.

So, I drove along, singing to the bees to calm them (and to calm me), and made it home in record time, where I spent twenty minutes or so coaxing two or three dozen bees out of my car's back window.

photo credit: Kara Dunn

And remember how I so confidently told you the way to remove the queen cage from the package, remove the cork from the end that had the candy plug in it, and hang the cage between two of the frames, so the queen and the workers could spend three or four days eating their way through the candy, thereby releasing the queen.

You remembered that, didn't you?

Well, I installed the queen cage in the hive body, dumped the 12,000 or so bees from the package into the hive, put the lid on, and THEN recalled that I hadn't taken out the cork.

After that, I put on my bee-jacket and veil. There was no way I was going back into that group of disgruntled critters without some protection. "Maybe," I thought, "they won't notice what I'm doing."

photo credit: Kara Dunn

They noticed. Did you ever try to pry a little cork out of a little hole while dozens of bees crawled around your hand wondering what you were doing?

I did get stung – once when I inadvertently squashed a bee between my hand and the screwdriver handle. And once when I squeezed another one between my hand and the knife handle. The screwdriver hadn't worked. It just pushed the cork farther into the hole, so I asked my neighbor (whose daughter was taking these wonderful pictures) to pop in to my kitchen (where I hadn't washed the dishes after my hurried breakfast) and bring me a sharp skinny knife.

That worked.

BeesKnees #2: A Beekeeping Memoir

Finally, everything was back in place. The bees settled in quite nicely before dark.

I'll have to go back into the hive in three or four days to remove the queen cage (assuming she's gotten out of it) and to be sure she's started laying eggs. I think I'd better wear my veil when I do it, just in case they remember the kook who:
- **cooped them up for a 3-hour drive**
- **dumped them into a big hive**
- **bothered them by opening the lid and poking around**
- **and then had the audacity to squash two of their sisters**

I do hope bees are forgiving.

Now, let's all celebrate.

BeeAttitude for Day #188: *Blessed are those who try their best, for we shall forgive and forget.*

One thing Fran is grateful for right now: *The full moon shining like a drop of liquid gold over the treetops as I drove toward Atlanta early Sunday morning.*

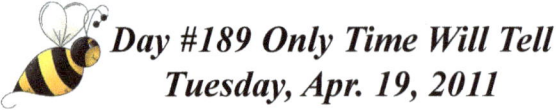
Day #189 Only Time Will Tell
Tuesday, Apr. 19, 2011

I hope the hive location on my deck is going to be okay for the bees. The trouble is that the house blocks the sunlight until about 9:30 in the morning. On Monday morning, when the sun hit the yellow hive (the one in which I installed the package of bees on Sunday), they woke right up and came streaming out into the daylight. Before that, I guess they were too chilly. But the white hive was still awfully quiet, so I moved it a foot or so to the side, closer to the yellow one, into the sunlight. Then those bees became a bit more active, but they're still not flying around as much as the yellow-hive bees.

Of course, once the true heat of summer has hit Georgia (and I do mean *hit*, because it can feel like a sledgehammer), then maybe the early morning shade from the house and the afternoon shade from the deciduous trees to the west will keep the bees from having to work so hard to cool the interior.

Only time will tell.

BeeAttitude for Day #189: *Blessed are children, for they shall lighten up the world.*

One thing Fran is grateful for right now: *My dental hygienist, who compliments me on my squeaky-clean teeth.*

Day #190 The Birds and the Bees and the Raccoons
Wednesday, Apr. 20, 2011

I've been feeding birds for decades, and they still fly off in fright whenever I open the door or step onto my porch. I don't mind that, since their instantaneous flight is a survival mechanism.

When I lived in Vermont, we used to feed the raccoons, who would trustingly come right up onto our deck. One even crawled into my lap one day. I do NOT recommend this. When I think of the length of his teeth as he examined my face, I get goose bumps. It was a stupid thing to do. But, like most twenty-somethings, I thought I was invincible.

The sad thing was, within two years those 22 raccoons we'd been feeding on a regular basis were gone. I'm sure that when we taught them not to be afraid of humans, they forgot their instinctive tendency to flee or hide, so 22 Vermont hunters soon sported raccoon tails in their dead animal collections. I regret that exceedingly, because the raccoons were so very trusting.

The bees don't fly away when I step onto the deck, nor do they even seem to pay much attention to me. But Tuesday I went out there to take out the two screws the H&L Bee Farm guy had used to make sure the lid wouldn't come off as I drove the bees home.

The bees let me take out the one at the back end of the hive. But when I stepped up to the front, to reach the one on the front edge, the guard bees simply were not happy with me. I got the screw about an eighth of an inch up, and then a guard bee bumped my head.

"Okay, ladies," I said. "We'll do this in increments."

I figure that if I can raise that screw one-eighth of an inch a day, it'll take me just a little more than a week to get it out.

I'm okay with that. Let them protect their hive. And stay safe.

BeeAttitude for Day #190: *Blessed are those who learn what we try to teach them, for we shall not sting them.*

One thing Fran is grateful for right now: *The filtered sunlight shining through the trees as I write.*

 ### Day #191 First Pollen Pocket
Thursday, Apr. 21, 2011

Photo credit: pexels.com (Pixabay)

Late Wednesday morning, as I sat next to the hives drinking a cup of tea, I saw a bee with those bright yellow "saddlebags" on her back legs, the corbiculae that I wrote about last October 25th on day #14 of this blog. Those pollen pockets had been, until Wednesday, only a vague concept to me. Now, the reality of those foragers carting load after load of nectar and pollen has come home to me in a flash of insight.

In the hours since that moment, of course, I've seen plenty more of them, and I'm gratified to know that the trees and flowers around here are providing plenty of protein for my honeybees.

But that very first sight of that very first bee will stand out in my memory for a long time. The wonder of that bright flash of golden yellow felt like a miracle. And, I suppose, it was.

BeeAttitude for Day #191: *Blessed are those who move slowly around our hives, for they shall see bee-wonders.*

One thing Fran is grateful for right now: *The stately crows who stride around my front yard*

Day #192 I Left the Queen Cage in Too Long
Friday, Apr. 22, 2011

My dear friend Nanette Littlestone, who also happens to be my editor and therefore helps bring order to my often chaotic manuscripts, asked if she could see the bees. "Sure," I said. "Come Thursday and you can help!"

So she dropped by that afternoon. The cage the queen bee came in needed to be removed, and I needed to replace that extra frame I'd taken out as I was installing the package. Nanette watched as I tried and tried and tried to light the smoker. She cheered when I finally managed the task. She stood back as I lifted the lid.

Oh, expletive! I'd left the queen cage in there too long because the bees had busily built two gorgeous sections of comb hanging down from the lid into the space I'd left open. Naturally, when I lifted the lid, that comb came up with it, covered by hundreds of working bees. They were stuffing it full of nectar and pollen. Much to my chagrin, as I discovered later – there were dozens (hundreds?) of teeny-tiny bee eggs in the comb as well.

If I'd lifted the empty cage out on Tuesday or Wednesday, I might have saved the lives of all those little eggs that now won't grow into beehood. I'm feeling really sad right now. I know I can't save every bee on the planet. I can't even save every bee in my own yard. But I sure do wish I could have foreseen this problem.

S I G H . . .

Of course, the good news is that, even though I didn't spot the queen herself, I have incontrovertible proof that she lives and thrives.

Maybe I'll just concentrate on that.

BeeAttitude for Day #192: *Blessed are those who understand how we work, for they shall find happiness in knowing.*

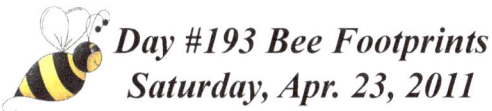 *Day #193 Bee Footprints*
Saturday, Apr. 23, 2011

You do recall, don't you, that the package bees went into the rubber-duck-yellow hive I'd bought way back last October? And that the fully-operative hive I brought home (along with the 3-pound package of bees) turned out to be white. Because that one has been functioning as a working hive for long enough for the bees to build up their comb and fill it with pollen and honey and eggs and larvae and pupae and those cute little emerging baby bees, there have been a lot of bee trips in and out of the front entrance, which is simply a hole about an inch in diameter.

As I sat watching the bees late yesterday afternoon, I noticed that the entrance hole on the yellow hive is still as bright yellow as the rest of the box, but the one on the white hive is – well – rather grungy-looking. It didn't take long to figure out that I was looking at countless bee footprints.

Imagine your kitchen floor, newly scrubbed. Now imagine a virtual horde of family members tromping in from outside, where they've been cavorting barefooted in the grass. And they each walk across the floor not once, not twice, but thousands of times.

Get the idea?

BeeAttitude for Day #193: *Blessed are our house bees, for they keep the hive cleaned out – except for the footprints, which we don't mind.*

One thing Fran is grateful for right now: *The leafy green of my back-deck potato plants growing up to the sun*

 ### Day #194 I wish my dad were here
Sunday, Apr. 24, 2011

Saturday, four of us from the Gwinnett Beekeepers Club staffed a table at Whole Foods for their celebration of Earth Day.

Photo credit: David Hablützel (pexels.com)

It was such fun talking with people who were in the same situation I was in last October – intrigued by bees, wanting to learn more, wondering if there were any way they could possibly raise bees.

Well, folks, I'm here to say that it is most definitely possible.

© Yelloideas Photography

I certainly hope that at least some of them will make the decision I did. Sitting here as I write this, looking out at the busy meanderings in front of the hive, I feel such a sense of peace and of accomplishment. I wish my dad were still alive so I could share this with him.

BeeAttitude for Day #194: *Blessed are the people who stop to ask questions, for they shall find awe-inspiring answers.*

One thing Fran is grateful for right now: *The hummingbirds gracing my three feeders*

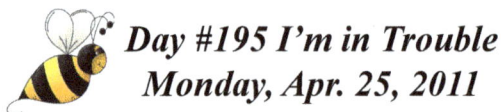 Day #195 I'm in Trouble
Monday, Apr. 25, 2011

I tried Sunday afternoon to open the white hive, just to check and be sure it wasn't time to put another layer on top so they could expand.

I lit the smoker without a hitch.

I used my hive tool to loosen the lid.

I lifted the lid about half an inch.

Whoops! It was way too heavy. I could see through the feeder hole on top that the frames were coming up along with the lid. Those busy little worker bees have glued the frames to the lid! I'd need about six hands in order to fix this problem.

You see, I'll HAVE to get the lid off eventually, because that will be the only way to make room for another hive body on top of this one. If I can't get the lid off, those bees are going to swarm when they begin to get too crowded, and that could be fairly soon.

"What did you do, Fran?"

I'm glad you asked. I settled the lid back down, hoping I wasn't squashing anybody. Then I sent out a panicked email to bee club members asking for help. Of course, it was Easter Sunday, so I figured I wouldn't hear from anyone that day. But I sure hope I hear soon.

I don't want to deal with a swarm this early in the season. In the meantime, I went and played for a while in the garden.

Photo credit: Ofer Dahan (pexels.com)

BeeAttitude for Day #195: *Blessed are those who answer questions or lend a hand, for they shall keep our beekeeper calm.*

One thing Fran is grateful for right now: *The lovely dinner I had at my daughter's house. I so enjoy being with them.*

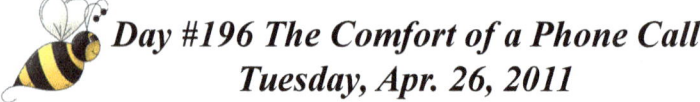 ### *Day #196 The Comfort of a Phone Call*
Tuesday, Apr. 26, 2011

Tommy Bailey, one of the founders of our Beekeepers Club, called me Monday afternoon in answer to the frantic email I'd sent out on Sunday.

He very patiently walked me through, step-by-step, the process for opening the white hive and correcting the problem. I'm going to tackle it today after I get home from giving blood. Send me some good thoughts, please. Tommy swears that I can do it, and I'm almost ready to believe him.

I'll let you know in Wednesday's blog.

Let's hope Tuesday stays sunny, so the bees won't be nervous.

BeeAttitude for Day #196: *Blessed are those who are brave enough to learn new skills, for they shall keep us bees entertained.*

What Fran is grateful for right now: *Tommy's encouragement*

Happy Birthday, Savannah!

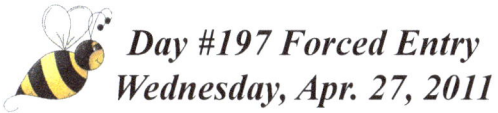
Day #197 Forced Entry
Wednesday, Apr. 27, 2011

When I suited up Tuesday to try to correct the problem in my white hive, I felt so much fear, my hands were trembling. The fear wasn't OF the bees. It was FOR the bees. What if I had somehow or other compromised the health of the hive? What if I had inadvertently squashed the queen? What if my nightmare from the night before had come true? What if the pine straw was so wet from Monday's rain that I wouldn't be able to get the smoker to stay lit?

"Get a grip, Frannie!"

Thank you, to whoever said that.

The smoker did light and stayed lit. The funniest thing was that, when I blew the smoke into the front door of the hive, I had the strongest impression of *calm,* and it felt like it was coming from the hive itself.

I'd noticed on Monday that they didn't seem to be drinking anything from their supplemental feeder jar (the one I'd given them when I couldn't get the lid off the first time), so I pulled it off and blew a bit more smoke down into that hole. Then I righted the jar, so nothing would drip out of the little holes – and I saw that there **weren't any** holes in the lid. I'd put the wrong lid on the jar when I was so discombobulated on Sunday.

It took me a longer time to pry up the lid far enough so that I could try to ease the hive tool under the overhang. I worked both ends loose first, being sure to stand at the SIDE of the hive, and not in front of it. As I've mentioned before, bees get nervous when someone stands in front of their door.

I went to the back of the hive again and lifted the top as far as I could, slipped the hive tool under it, gave the tiniest little push, and BANG! Whatever had been stuck let go and crashed back into the hive. Fortunately, it had only about an inch to fall, but that one inch almost scared the you-know-what right out of me.

I couldn't believe my good luck that the whole thing hadn't been cemented with propolis. Still, I tried hard to quash the fear that somehow that dreadful crash might have damaged the queen.

With great trepidation I lifted the lid and saw . . .
a wonderful working thriving hive

Can you imagine the relief I felt? Of course, I still had to be sure the queen was in there somewhere, so I lifted out one of the frames. It had a few bees on it, but no comb to speak of. That meant there was still room for the hive to expand before I'd need to put a second layer on top.

Frame Perch from Brushy Mountain Bee Farm Catalog

The second frame was harder to lift, mainly because it was covered with bees, although it didn't have more than half the area covered in drawn-out comb yet, and I didn't spot a queen in there. Thank goodness for the frame perch I bought. As you can see from this picture from the **Brushy Mountain website**, it's a sturdy metal thing-a-ma-bob with two brackets that slip over the side of the hive body. The two long pieces that stick out to the side are perfect for setting the frames on after inspection. The perch made it easy for me to keep the frames in order.

Next I pulled up the middle frame – and there was a **queen** with a long, fat abdomen. She scurried a bit, probably looking for some dark recess, so I set that frame back in place.

I checked the two remaining frames, replaced the ones I'd taken out, and closed up the hive.

I didn't look for any larvae or eggs. I didn't register the ration of capped brood to capped honey. I didn't notice whether there were any drone cells. Oh well, at least I know I have a queen in there, and the other bees are happy.

Life is good, indeed, and all is well.

BeeAttitude for Day #197: *Blessed are those who hear our messages, for they shall be comforted.*

One thing Fran is grateful for right now: *Those of you who read my blog*

Day #198 Probably a False Alarm
Thursday, Apr. 28, 2011

I'm writing this on Wednesday afternoon, hoping to get it scheduled before the storms hit and (possibly) the power goes out. Tornados are predicted, although there have been so many false alarms lately it's hard to take the prediction seriously.

All morning long the weather was relatively clear, and the bees acted the way they usually do. But at 4:00 the sky clouded over ominously and the wind picked up. I noticed swirling masses of bees around the entrances to both hives. It looked like every forager bee had decided to come home and get inside–all of them at the same time. Sort of like rush hour in Atlanta, with seven lanes of interstate packed solid.

I'm going to post this really fast so I can unplug everything and wait out the storm.

All will be well, I'm sure. I just hope the bees aren't in too much of a tizzy. But it does look like they know something I don't.

BeeAttitude for Day #198: *Blessed are those who pay attention to the world around them, for they shall be prepared.*

One thing Fran is grateful for right now: *The teeny, teeny blueberries on the bushes I planted last month.*

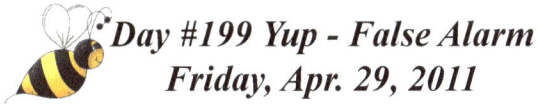
Day #199 Yup - False Alarm
Friday, Apr. 29, 2011

This is the last time I'll get worried when the bees start congregating around the hive entrance. Nothing came of the severe weather warnings except for some high winds and fairly spectacular lightning around midnight. I got up and sat by the window for a while, watching the show and counting the seconds before the thunderclap. Nothing hit within two miles of my house.

I wish the same were true for those families in Alabama and elsewhere who were devastated by the storms. I truly wish them well in their recovery efforts.

So, what were the bees trying to tell me at 4 in the afternoon? I haven't a clue. I think I'm going to have to watch the bees a lot more carefully and chart their behavior patterns before I'll know what (if anything) they're predicting.

When I find out, I'll let you know.

BeeAttitude for Day #199: *Blessed are they who listen to us bees, for we have much to tell them. We just wish you humans could speak* **BEEnglish**.

One thing Fran is grateful for right now: *The right of free speech*

 *Day #200 1/3 of the way there*
Saturday, Apr. 30, 2011

When I started this blog last October, I pledged to write daily for 600 days. Today's post is the end of the first third of that project.

Let's **celebrate** with a bee joke:

How do you hug a bee?

p.s. Bill & Billy - I already have your answer, but you can send another one if you want to.

BeeAttitude for Day #200: *Blessed are those who fulfill their promises, for they shall sleep peacefully.*

One thing Fran is grateful for right now: *Warm fuzzy slippers*

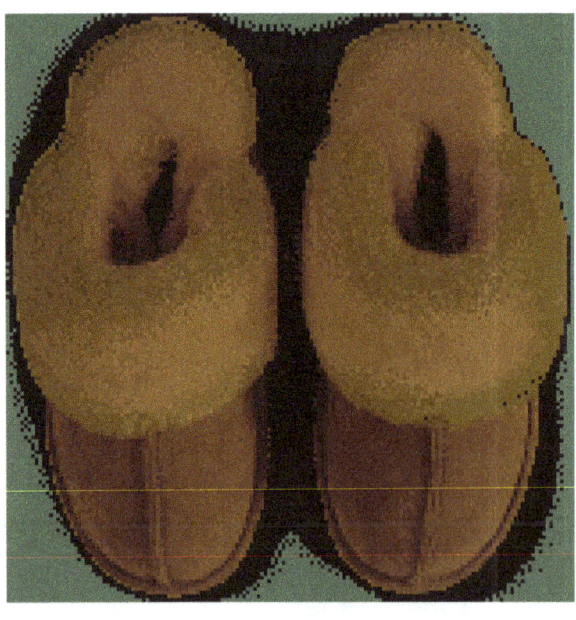

A Final Note for Now:
Once this process is completed, there will "bee" six volumes of the BeesKnees Memoirs.

I hope you'll stick with me through the entire journey.

--Fran

www.ingramcontent.com/pod-product-compliance
Lightning Source LLC
Chambersburg PA
CBHW071712020426
42333CB00017B/2231

Praise

Groce explores what it truly means to be a leader in the modern world. His discussions on the presidency and leadership are insightful and will resonate with anyone interested in public service.
Mike Lipkin | President, Motivational Speaker & Coach

We Have Nothing to Lose: A Dark Optimist's Call to Action is a rallying cry for those ready to take life into their own hands, embrace their power, and confront challenges head-on. Ralph H. Groce III delivers an urgent roadmap for tackling some of the most complex challenges of our time, igniting a bold vision of what's possible when we refuse to accept limits on our collective potential.
Dr. Karida Brown | NAACP Image Award-winning Author and Professor of Sociology, Emory University

Ralph's discussions on the presidency and leadership are insightful and will resonate with anyone interested in public service.
Ibrahim Jackson | Founder & CEO

Groce cleverly weaves the frank and often demoralizing reality of life with an optimism that is uncloaked and raw, which makes his calls to action feel not just correct but also doable. Inspirational and motivating, Groce presents a new framework for living that is eye-to-eye with the reader, achieving an inclusivity that truly any reader will experience, and benefit from.
Devin Bramhall | Growth Advisor

The book is well balanced in that Ralph talks about the power of technology, achieving positive results even though there were many obstacles and having a vision and commitment to improve the world that we live in. Well done.
Lester Owens | Senior Executive Vice President Head of Operations

In an era marked by doubt and division, this book challenges readers to embrace personal accountability, offering a transformative perspective on collective healing. More than a book, it's a potential catalyst for a much-needed social movement—inviting each of us to be architects of meaningful change and to join a collective committed to making the world a healthier place for all.

Mary Schaub | Founder & CEO

This book strikes the perfect balance between hope and realism. Ralph H. Groce doesn't promise easy solutions, but he offers practical tools and insights for anyone who's ready to make a change.

Cathy Anderson | Author, Professor and Consultant

The author's take on how technology can be harnessed for good is incredibly hopeful. Groce offers a compelling vision of a future where innovation drives progress for all.

William Sparks Ph.D. | David Thompson Chair and Professor of Leadership

The book the world needs right now. Groce uses personal reflections to explore the big political, social, and environmental challenges humanity faces in the 21st century. This thought-provoking read will keep you thinking longer after you've finished a reading. If you are searching for hope and inspiration - this book is a must read!

Dr. Dani Chesson | Founder & Director

A prescient look at the existential problems our society is facing and a strong appeal to leverage our knowledge and moral strength to move ahead. This book is a remarkable tale about personal and professional growth and commitment to bold action and finding solutions to new unprecedented challenges.

Tanya Zlateva Ph.D. | Dean & Professor of the Practice of Computer Science and Education

In this book, *We Have Nothing to Lose,* Ralph Groce confronts pessimism with dark optimism and brilliance. This work is frank, bold, and audacious, challenging the status quo and politics, as is typical of someone who has